MW00974257

ADVANCED AUTOHYPNOSIS

Provides a thorough investigation into what self-hypnosis is
and the reasons for its effectiveness.

ADVANCED AUTO-HYPNOSIS

by

Ronald Shone

THORSONS PUBLISHERS LIMITED
Wellingborough, Northamptonshire

First published 1985

British Library Cataloguing in Publication Data

Shone, R. (Ronald)
    Advanced autohypnosis.
    1. Autogenic training
    I. Title
    154.7'6   RC499.A8

    ISBN 0-7225-0881-6

Printed and bound in Great Britain

Acknowledgement

The author wishes to express his thanks to his wife, Anne Thomson, for her incisive comments on many of the earlier chapters of this book. If her own work had not taken her abroad no doubt the later chapters would have been much improved by the same incisive comments. As it is, the author claims sole responsibility.

Contents

Introduction

In recent years hypnosis has been gaining in popularity, not least because it is now more understood than ever before. This does not mean that we know exactly what it is, but it does mean that its mystery has become somewhat less. Part of the growing appreciation of hypnosis has come from the benefits which can be derived from autohypnosis: from engaging in self-hypnosis. If one reads many of the works on hypnosis the overriding majority concentrate on heterohypnosis, that is the act of one person hypnotizing another. The reader would not be far wrong in drawing the conclusion from many of these works that *all* hypnosis was heterohypnosis. But, if anything, the opposite is the case: all hypnosis is autohypnosis. The hypnotist is doing no more than teaching the person being hypnotized how to enter a hypnotic state. It is a process which must be learnt.

The present author considers that there is nothing fundamentally different between heterohypnosis and autohypnosis, therefore both are considered in this book. However, the emphasis is on aspects of autohypnosis which have generally been neglected, or not considered at all. It is for this reason that familiar topics of hypnosis are considered, but they are considered in terms of what light they shed on a person undertaking autohypnosis. This appears justified because the potential and benefits of autohypnosis have generally gone unrecognized.

Emphasis of the Book
The book has three main features which it emphasizes:

1. Positive and negative hypnosis. It is indicated that the first

activates the parasympathetic nervous system, while the latter activates the sympathetic nervous system.

2. Features of the right and left hemispheres of the brain, and how such functional specialization has given us some insights into the hypnotic state.

3. Altered states of consciousness, arguing that hypnosis is simply one particular altered state but as yet not clearly delineated from other altered states.

These three features run throughout virtually the whole of the book. However, the first and second are dealt with in detail in Chapter 2, and the third in Chapter 3. Although this material is more technical than the usual discussions of hypnosis, it is felt that a deeper understanding of the scientific basis of the hypnotic phenomenon will take away much of the mystery which still surrounds it. Although the book certainly does have this 'scientific' bent to it, the emphasis is still on the use of autohypnosis for self-improvement.

An Overview

Chapter 1 presents a brief history of hypnosis. In this chapter the debate between the Nancy school and the Salpêtrière Institute is highlighted because of the light it sheds on positive and negative hypnosis. Chapter 2 is probably the most technical of all. It discusses the nervous system, particularly the brain and a number of the brain's structures. The aim of this chapter is two-fold. First, to present what is known about the nervous system to date – at least those aspects of the nervous system which have a bearing on hypnosis. Second, to present a number of conjectures in the light of these modern researches.

Chapter 3 presents a discussion of consciousness, particularly altered states of consciousness (ASC). Research on ASCs has shed much light on the workings of the mind and especially its non-linear features. It is now generally accepted that the left hemisphere of the brain operates in a linear mode (logically and rationally, going from A to B to C), while the right hemisphere of the brain operates in a non-linear mode (seeing things as a whole, holistically). This research, as Chapter 3 makes clear, sheds much light on the hypnotic state. It also gives some idea of why autohypnosis is within everyone's grasp and can be achieved by almost anyone. At the same time, this chapter reveals what is *not* known about hypnosis.

Chapters 4 and 5 turn to more traditional topics in hypnosis. Chapter 4 deals with the correlation between personality and hypnosis. Although this research has many shortcomings, largely because of the difficulty in quantifying both personality and hypnosis, it does shed some light on the hypnotic state. The same is true of studies on the depth of hypnosis, which is discussed in Chapter 5. Hypnotic depth is particularly of interest to the scientist, but also for the self-hypnotist who is concerned whether their depth is great enough. What is emphasized here is that there can be too much concentration on depth. Furthermore, what matters in autohypnosis is why you are engaging in it, and not going as deep as possible.

In Chapter 6, on 'The Principles of Autohypnosis', an attempt is made to bring together what might be called 'principles'. Although many of these principles have been applied to suggestions and, most particularly, have been applied to heterohypnosis, they certainly do apply to auto-hypnosis. One feature of this chapter is a more thorough discussion of the principles than is usually presented. The three 'laws' of suggestion may be called 'laws', but they are far from self-evident and they certainly require explaining. The chapter concludes with a discussion of the meaning of 'rapport' in the case of autohypnosis.

Chapter 7 presents a discussion of the relationship between autohypnosis and a number of related subjects, such as biofeedback, meditation, yoga, religion and faith-healing.

It will be noted that no mention has been made of techniques. This is because the emphasis of the book is explanatory. It is attempting to provide some scientific insight into autohypnosis as far as the developments in science will allow. It must be emphasized that these are largely conjectural because at the present time we simply do not know what hypnosis is. There are a number of theories on what it is but no generally accepted one. However, modern brain research has considerably increased our insight into the phenomenon of hypnosis and this insight does provide some basis for the greater potential of autohypnosis than has previously been thought.

The standard techniques, both of heterohypnosis and autohypnosis, are usually undertaken with the eyes closed.

However, the present investigation indicates that it is possible to be in autohypnosis even with the eyes open. The difference is simply a matter of degree. Retaining autohypnosis with the eyes open requires more training. There is nothing in the set of principles, highlighted in Chapter 6, which precludes auto-hypnosis with the eyes open. How to achieve this is presented in Chapter 8 – this being the only advanced 'technique' that is required.

1.
History and Theory
of Autohypnosis

Reviewing the history of any subject is always useful in putting it into perspective. This is especially true of hypnosis. In this chapter, however, the intention is to present a rather selective view of the subject. Attention will constantly be focused on what insights the developments give us about autohypnosis. As we shall see in a moment, in the early days of the subject all hypnosis was heterohypnosis. Even so, looking at these developments gives us some insight into the state of hypnosis itself.

We shall divide the period into three phases which we have labelled:

- – Animal magnetism.
- – The period of controversy.
- – The rise of psychoanalysis.

Animal Magnetism

Although hypnosis in some form has been known about since the beginning of recorded history, it took on new significance with the presentation of Anton Mesmer's dissertation in 1766. He argued that the planets, in addition to affecting each other, also influenced all organized bodies – including man – through their effects on the fluid which occupies all space. This became known as animal magnetism. The emphasis on magnetism is important. It was thought at the time that the hypnotist, with the aid of magnets, could place a person in a trance. It must be appreciated that at the time magnetism was topical and 'scientific'. The force was known about and, more to the point, was invisible. This hypothesis was totally incorrect but it set the trend for almost the next one hundred years.

When putting patients into a trance Mesmer would touch them with iron magnets. Soon he realized that he did not need magnets as such, as any magnetized object would do. He magnetized the objects by passing his hands over them (no doubt in the presence of his patients). Later he used a magnetized 'wand' and even a tree. When touched, many of his patients went into various states of limb catalepsy, convulsions, comas, speaking in strange voices etc., – all of which we would now refer to as hysteria.

This observation itself is most important. Today such hysterical response does not occur. Why was this the typical response in the time of Mesmer but not today? This is a difficult question to answer but there are two interrelated reasons. First, because it was considered that the trance was brought on by a magnetic force and that this was the 'right' response to such a force. The argument being advanced here is that people considered that this was the 'typical' trance state: this is what a person did when in a trance. (In different cultures, and at different times in history, people have responded with what they thought was the 'typical' response for that culture or that time.) A second reason, which we shall clarify in the next chapter, is that the trance states created at the time of Mesmer were largely negative hypnotic states rather than the positive state produced today. Briefly, a negative hypnotic state is created by activating the sympathetic nervous system while a positive hypnotic state activates the parasympathetic nervous system. (The sympathetic and parasympathetic nervous systems will be discussed in the next chapter.) A very active sympathetic nervous system is typical of hysteria. Hysteria and the sympathetic nervous system interrelate in the sense that a cataleptic state could only be achieved by activating the sympathetic nervous system.

A second observation immediately arises. If we discount the hypothesis that the magnets had anything to do with the trance state, then what, or who, activated the patients' sympathetic nervous system? It was, of course, the patients themselves. This, to some extent, was recognized by the Royal Commission of Inquiry which was set up in 1784 to investigate animal magnetism. They saw no evidence to support the hypothesis that animal magnetism was in any way involved. They were of the opinion, however, that the imagination was a major factor in the response of patients.

Although Mesmer was totally mistaken about magnetism he did note that it was important to establish a good relationship between patient and physician. This he called *rapport*, a term used to this day. As was noted much later, rapport is the situation in which the patient has confidence and belief in what the physician says; in other words, the suggestions of the hypnotist are more likely to be carried out. This observation is most important for the autohypnotist. It appears to be a human disposition to accept authority and experts, certainly far more readily than oneself. (It is common for students to believe that what they read is correct because it has been published, even if they do not agree with what is being said. Very few have confidence to assert that they are correct and the book – the expert – is wrong.) When engaging in self-hypnosis, therefore, it is essential to have confidence in one's ability to achieve success. Put another way, the auto-hypnotist must find a substitute for the rapport which is established in heterohypnosis. Belief in the hypnotic state, and confidence in one's ability to achieve it, is the essential ingredient for success in autohypnosis.

One of the first to break with the idea of animal magnetism and realize that suggestion was all that was required was the Abbé Faria. He engaged in producing trance states as an act to obtain money (just as was to occur in the theatres). In his performances he simply suggested in a quiet but authoritative voice that a person should go to 'sleep'. Somnambulists (the most responsive of hypnotic subjects) did so. He was, however, discredited by an actor who pretended to be hypnotized.

Another major change, and a break with animal magnetism, occurred in Britain. James Braid, a Scottish surgeon working in Manchester, dispensed with the idea of a fluid in which people are purported to exist, and demonstrated that the trance state could be achieved by holding a bright object a little above the subject's eye line. Why did he use this method? He likened the sleep of animal magnetism to natural sleep. Since, he reasoned, natural sleep occurs when a person is fatigued then why not the mesmeric trance? He reasoned that it was fatigue that brought on hypnosis and not magnetism. His experiments appeared to verify his hypothesis. It was he who introduced the word 'hypnosis'. Of course, Braid too was mistaken; it was not fatigue but a case of suggestion and belief. The link with fatigue, just like the link with magnetism, was spurious. However, the abandonment of animal magnetism as the force in the trance state was now becoming more widespread.

Before leaving this period of history one other comment is in order. The many experiments being undertaken at the time (largely in France, and then later in other parts of Europe) noted other features of the hypnotic state – in particular, clairvoyance. This was unfortunate. A large part of the interest was in clairvoyance and not in the trance state. One typical case is that of the Chastenet de Puységur. A believer in animal magnetism himself, he came across a somnambulist named Victor. Under hypnosis, he got Victor to diagnose other people's disorders. Very soon hypnosis and travelling clairvoyance were being combined. I shall not go into these links in this book (but see Edmunds,[10]). All that is being pointed out is that by combining them it became difficult to disentangle one from the other. However, these particular experiments did supply one important observation on the hypnotic state itself. They all illustrated that hypnosis involves heightened awareness of a number of the senses. This is an important observation in its own right, especially because a number of commentators who know very little about hypnosis tend to deny this fact. There is no need to accept clairvoyance and other paranormal phenomena associated with hypnosis to accept heightened awareness of the senses.

The Period of Controversy
Braid's approach to hypnosis became known on the Continent when, three days before his death, a paper of his was read to the French Academy. At this meeting was a French country doctor, A. A. Liébeault, who had a practice just outside Nancy. He returned to his practice with the intention of trying Braid's methods. He would treat his patients with the usual methods employing drugs at the standard charge, but would treat them with hypnosis for nothing. He simply suggested to his patients very quietly that they were ready to go to sleep, and many of them did so. They did not fall into a natural sleep but rather into a hypnotic trance. When in this trance he would give them suggestions, again in a very quiet voice, which would help them in removing their symptoms. In his view, it was the suggestions when made in this state which were important and not the means of achieving the hypnotic state.

This was probably the clearest change from negative to positive hypnosis (although this distinction was not made then – or now to a very great extent). The use of quiet suggestion activated the parasympathetic nervous system and produced a trance state that was calm rather than hysterical.

The same technique, following on from Braid, was used by M. Charcot, Professor at the Salpêtrière in Paris. He, however, was dealing with hysterics and was of the opinion that hypnosis was a heightened neuro-muscular state and akin to epilepsy, but artificially induced. Charcot's patients all exhibited the cataleptic state we discussed above and basically were exhibiting negative hypnosis. In terms of the history of the subject, Charcot provided an explanation for the hypnotic state. Once animal magnetism was abandoned the trance state, although plain to see, could not be accounted for. Charcot argued that it was a neurological condition. But there was an unfortunate element in his analysis. The neurological condition, he argued, was in fact a disorder: it was hystero-epilepsy which was artificially induced. It was not, therefore, difficult to see the next step in the logic. As a disorder it should not be induced – except possibly to investigate hysteria. Accordingly, there was no need for doctors to learn hypnosis. In simple terms the assertion was that anyone who went into a hypnotic state was in a temporary state of hysteria!

Charcot's analysis illustrates the danger of generalizing from a limited sample. His patients were all hysterics to begin with (the Salpêtrière was a sanatorium) and all went into negative hypnosis. It was not surprising, therefore, that Charcot concluded that hypnosis was akin to hysteria. Whether an individual is under hypnosis or not, a highly active sympathetic nervous system generally produces the same effects. Thus, having abandoned the link between hypnosis and magnetism, there was now a link between hypnosis and hysteria – a link which did not help the development of hypnosis.

Fortunately for hypnosis, an alternative hypothesis was advanced by the Nancy School which was in sharp contrast to the Salpêtrière. In 1882 Liébeault had cured a patient of Professor H. Bernheim. Bernheim was so impressed that he introduced hypnosis into his own hospital at Nancy. Obviously, he followed the methods of Liébeault who in turn based his on Braid. We have made the point that Braid's method was basically a stimulation of the parasympathetic nervous system through quiet suggestions. This positive hypnotic state bore very little resemblance to the negative hypnotic state that was being produced at Salpêtrière. Unfortunately, Liébeault took a retrogressive step in going back to animal magnetism. At the same time, a student of Charcot's re-awakened the debate over related mental achievements in the hypnotic state. More significant was his hypothesis that hypnosis could not simply be a mechanical act, as Charcot had asserted. The point was whether these accounts were examples of hyperacuity or whether there really was something which passed between the hypnotist and the subject. So the debate was re-opened.

Charcot's interpretation was readily taken up at the outset, largely because it fitted into orthodox medicine as it was then known. But within four years it was generally discredited and evidence mounted for the Nancy School interpretation. Although many experimenters accepted the Nancy view, it was not acceptable to scientists. Why? This view was based on the idea of suggestion. Suggestion was a psychological state, and psychology at the time was not a well-defined, or a very credible, subject then. It would not, therefore, fit into the general orthodox approach of medicine. As far as scientists were concerned, therefore, the Salpêtrière supremacy had not been toppled. The controversy continued, each citing the same evidence in support of their theories. For instance, the stigmata of Louise Lateau (these were purported to be the same wounds as those of Christ) were cited in support by both schools . At the Nancy School the stigmata could be created by suggestion under hypnosis; while in the Salpêtrière the stigmata were taken to be another symptom of hystero-epilepsy.

However, evidence was mounting that suggestion did play an important role in hypnosis. It was at this time that it was discovered that blisters could be formed by suggestion alone. In addition, healing could be speeded up in certain cases. This raised a problem for medical doctors. If the Salpêtrière view was correct then they need not learn hypnosis. If the Nancy School was correct, and if healing could be speeded up, then they would have to learn hypnosis.

One important observation which is not generally recognized comes out of this discussion and that is: *both were probably correct*. If we accept, as we shall argue in the next chapter, that both positive and negative hypnosis can exist, then the Salpêtrière were dealing with negative hypnosis and argued their case from that point of view; the Nancy School were dealing with positive hypnosis and were arguing their case from this point of view. Both have elements of truth, but neither is an explanation of all aspects of hypnosis. In so far as the therapeutic aspects of hypnosis come from positive hypnosis, there is a leaning today towards the Nancy view. But the discussion of this debate also illustrates the different approaches we observe today. In some circles (and in some stage performances) it is the negative hypnotic state which is induced rather than the positive.

The Rise of Psychoanalysis

The next stage was associated with the rise in the psychoanalytic method, associated most with Sigmund Freud. Hypnosis had reached the situation where it was being used as a direct method of symptom removal and was not dealing with the cause of the problem. The psychoanalytic movement pioneered by Freud was to concentrate on the causes and not simply on symptom removal. In fact, Freud's ideas began with an observation he made when visiting the clinic of Liébeault and Bernheim at Nancy in 1889. At about the same time, Breuer was eliminating the symptoms of hysteria by an indirect method. Whilst in a hypnotic state, he got his patients to verbalize their problems. The two men began a collaboration. But Freud later rejected hypnosis as a method of treatment and developed in its place the psychoanalytic method which was based on free association and dreams.

As Freud was developing his psychoanalytic method, interest in hypnosis continued at Nancy but it now took on a different approach based on the work of Emile Coué. Like Freud, Coué became interested in hypnosis after seeing the work of Liébeault. His main ideas, however, were made popular by Baudouin (just as Liébeault's ideas were made popular by Bernheim). The ideas of the New Nancy School, as it became known, were set out in Baudouin's *Suggestion and Autosuggestion*[3]. In brief, the New Nancy School argued that the main factor in hypnosis was autosuggestion; that the law of reverse effect (see chapter 6) was most important; and that the main aspects of autosuggestion occurred at the subconscious level. These developments, although not inconsistent with psychoanalysis, were overshadowed by the latter. They did, however, indicate that self-hypnosis was possible. Until this time all hypnosis had been heterohypnosis – largely because it was believed that it must be induced by someone else. If, as the New Nancy School were arguing, hypnosis involves autosuggestion then heterohypnosis is simply one form it can take. There should, in principle, be no difficulty in a person inducing hypnosis in themselves if they believe in it sufficiently.

A resurgence of interest in hypnosis arose during the First World War when there was need for a quicker cure for wartime neuroses. Hypnosis was found to be most effective in relieving symptoms by reliving war experiences. The same, in fact, was also true during and after the Second World War and the Korean war.[1, 15]

All these developments considered hypnosis as a *method* of dealing with psychological problems – what we now call hypnotherapy. In this book we are concerned with hypnosis itself and not hypnosis as a means of therapy. But put in historical perspective these developments led to the work of C. L. Hull and M. H. Erickson. Hull published his *Hypnosis and Suggestibility*[22] in 1933 and this in particular laid down the framework for the scientific investigation of hypnosis and related phenomena.

In 1953 the British Medical Association finally gave hypnosis its seal of approval – even suggesting that it be included in courses in psychiatry (and possibly given to obstetricians and anaesthetists). The Hypnosis Act of 1952 aided in reducing the misuse of hypnosis for entertainment. Even so, the subject is still associated with clairvoyance and other subject areas. The therapeutic act of age regression (i.e., under hypnosis being taken back to an earlier period of the person's life) has been taken to extremes and used to argue for reincarnation and previous lives. (The most conspicuous being Moss and Keeton[31]).

A more recent development, however, could prove to be most important in establishing what hypnosis is. Research into split brain patients has led to considerable insight into how the brain functions and processes information. It also gives us some insight as to the meaning of consciousness and altered states of consciousness, some of which we shall discuss in chapter 3. But as yet these developments are too new to give us any clear perspective on how they will change our views about hypnosis.

Conclusion

What can we conclude from the foregoing historical survey? We know hypnosis occurs but do not have an adequate (certainly not a generally accepted) theory of it. From a neuro-physical point of view it can occur when either the sympathetic (negative hypnosis) or the parasympathetic (positive hypnosis) nervous system is stimulated. It is closely associated with suggestion, especially when given by someone else (hetero-hypnosis) but can occur when the suggestions are given by oneself (autohypnosis). The autohypnotist must have a belief in the state and that he has the ability to bring it about. This is a substitute for *rapport* which can exist between subject and hypnotist in heterohypnosis.

The difficulty that some people have in going into hypnosis, whether self-induced or induced by someone else, probably has much to do with the person's need to keep in touch with reality (i.e., with the difficulty in 'letting go'). Recent developments of split brain patients are only just giving us insights into consciousness and its reality-testing, as against less conscious activities which are largely undertaken by the right hemisphere of the brain. In the coming chapters we shall pursue these recent developments.

2.
The Nervous System

This chapter has two main purposes. One is to lay down some of the more technical aspects of the nervous system which are important in coming to a deeper understanding of hypnosis. It will present, in simple terms, what is presently known about certain aspects of the nervous system. The second purpose is more conjectural and attempts to relate this information to our knowledge of hypnosis. It must be appreciated that our knowledge of the nervous system, and especially the brain, is very inadequate. At the same time, we do not know what hypnosis is. It follows, therefore, that any statements made about the importance of certain organs or functions in relation to hypnosis must be taken as conjecture.

In the first section we present an overview of the nervous system. This will allow the more selective aspects, which will be dealt with in later sections, to be seen in relation to the whole. The emphasis of this first section will be a discussion of the sympathetic and parasympathetic nervous systems. The second section deals with the brain. Three topics are covered: the three systems of the brain; the hemispherical division of the brain; and brainwaves. The final section deals with the importance of three organs (or more strictly, four) of the brain: the corpus callosum; the thalamus and hypothalamus; and the hippocampus.

An Overview of the Nervous System
Nerves are spread throughout the body to sense receptors (eyes, ears, nose and mouth), skin, muscles and internal organs. The nervous system although very interrelated can be sub-divided as shown in Figure 1.

The somatic system carries messages to and from the sense

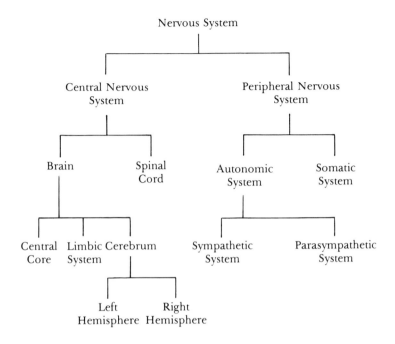

Figure 1

receptors, muscles and the surface of the body. It is this system which makes us aware of pain, pressure and temperature changes. All involuntary movements of muscles which deal with balance and posture are also carried by the nerves of the somatic system. In other words, the somatic system relays information to the brain about the body, in relation to the environment in which it finds itself. On the other hand, the autonomic nervous system consists of the nerves which connect internal organs to the central nervous system and regulate especially glands, respiration, heart-rate and digestion. Furthermore, the autonomic nervous system plays a major role in emotion. It is referred to as autonomic because many of its activities are automatic and self-regulatory. For instance, you continue to digest food when asleep and your heart continues beating without you being consciously aware of it. The autonomic nervous system, therefore, relays information about the state and internal workings of the body.

The nerves of the peripheral nervous system link up to the spinal cord, which is the main centre for conducting information up to the brain. The brain itself lies at the top of the spinal cord. The structure of the brain is usefully divided into three concentric layers (forming a lateral division of the brain): the central core brain, the limbic system and the cerebrum. In evolutionary terms, this is also the way the brain has developed. The core brain and limbic system control all reflexes while the cerebrum, which developed much later in evolution, and is contained only in higher vertebrates, is the centre of nonreflexive mental processes, e.g., thinking and reasoning. Of special importance in the core brain is the reticular activating system (commonly called RAS), which acts as mediator between the lower brain and the cortex. The cerebrum (sometimes referred to as the cerebral cortex, or simply the cortex for short) itself is composed of two hemispheres, called the left and right hemispheres, which are separated by a bundle of nerves called the corpus callosum.

The autonomic nervous system is divided into two parts: the sympathetic, and the parasympathetic. The system as a whole controls the glands and the smooth muscles – that is to say the muscles of the heart, blood vessels and the stomach (as distinct from those muscles connected to the skeleton). The sympathetic nervous system is composed of two main chains of nerves on either side of the spinal column from which connections are made to various organs in the chest, stomach and lower abdomen. The parasympathetic nervous system is composed largely of two parts. One part has nerve fibres arising from the upper part of the brain stem and a second part has nerves emanating from the lower region of the brain stem. About eighty per cent or more of the parasympathetic nerve fibres are in the upper portion which pass to the chest and stomach.

Although something of an over-exaggeration, it is possible to think of the two systems as influencing the body in opposite ways. When each system is stimulated the result is to excite some organs and to have inhibitory effects on others. More significantly, when sympathetic stimulation tends to excite a particular organ, parasympathetic stimulation tends to inhibit it. It is the case, however, that most organs are largely controlled by one or other of the two systems and so, in general, the two systems do not oppose each other. But even this is too simplistic. In a number of cases the two systems act together, and in still other cases they act in sequence. The interrelationship between the sympathetic and parasympathetic nervous systems is not yet fully understood. What has been established is the effects on various organs of excitation of each of the systems. These are given in Table 1.

Table 1

Autonomic Effects on Various Organs of the Body

Organ	Effect of Sympathetic Stimulation	Effect of Parasympathetic Stimulation
Eye: Pupil	Dilated	Constricted
Ciliary muscle	None	Excited
Glands:		
Nasal	Vasoconstriction	Stimulation of thin
Lacrimal		copious secretion
Parotid		containing many
Submaxillary		enzymes
Gastric		
Pancreatic		
Sweat glands	Copious sweating	None
Apocrine glands	Thick, oderiferous secretion	None
Heart: Muscle	Increased rate Increased rate of beat	Slowed rate Decreased force of atrial beat
Coronaries	Vasodilated	Constricted
Lungs: Bronchi	Dilated	Constricted
Blood vessels	Mildly constricted	None
Gut: Lumen	Decreased peristalsis and tone	Increased peristalsis and tone
Sphincter	Increased tone	Decreased tone
Liver	Glucose released	None
Gall bladder and bile ducts	Inhibited	Excited
Kidney	Decreased output	None
Ureter	Inhibited	Excited
Bladder: Detrusor	Inhibited	Excited
Trigone	Excited	Inhibited
Penis	Ejaculation	Erection
Systematic blood vessel:		
Abdomenal	Constricted	None
Muscle	Constricted (adrenergic) Dilated (cholinergic)	None

Organ	Effect of Sympathetic Stimulation	Effect of Parasympathetic Stmulation
Skin	Constricted (adrenergic) Dilated (cholinergic)	Dilated
Blood: Coagulation	Increased	None
Glucose	Increased	None
Basal metabolism	Increased (up to 150%)	None
Adrenal cortical secretion	Increased	None
Mental activity	Increased	None
Piloerector muscles	Excited	None

Source: Guyton, A.C. (1972) *Structure and Function of the Nervous System*

It can be seen from Table 1 that the sympathetic system will. when a person is emotionally excited, bring about an increase in heart-rate, dilation of the arteries of the muscles of the heart, constriction of the arteries of the skin and digestive organs, so leading to perspiration and the increase in emotional arousal. On the other hand, when the parasympathetic system is ároused the pupils contract, the heart-rate slows down, breathing slows down (as constriction of the bronchi takes place) and the skin dilates. (Notice also that there is an erection of the penis – an experience common for the male in the first stages of hypnosis. The dilation of the skin explains why many people experience a tingling sensation, especially in their arms and legs, when entering hypnosis.)

One difference between the two systems, which is of importance for hypnosis, is that the sympathetic nervous system affects a variety of organs *simultaneously*, while the parasympathetic nervous system tends to operate *one organ at a time*. Since the parasympathetic nervous system mainly affects chest and stomach, the system can be activated by concentrating on these areas. Concentration on slow rhythmic breathing will activate the parasympathetic nervous system as far as the chest is concerned. The stomach is a little harder, but concentrating on a warm glow in the navel region of the stomach can activate the parasympathetic nervous system in that area.

So far in this chapter we have made only a passing reference to hypnosis. Now let me turn to some conjectures in the light of the discussion so far. In the first chapter we noted the difference of opinion on hypnosis between the Salpêtrière and the Nancy School. The work at the Salpêtrière was on schizophrenics. Such subjects are usually emotionally aroused, can create catatonic states, and show general hysterical symptoms associated with a highly activated sympathetic nervous system. When the sympathetic system is very aroused then the body takes on a fight or flight condition. Action is almost reflexive and spontaneous. In other words, when the sympathetic nervous system is aroused conscious thought processes are largely bypassed. But this is one of the main requirements for inducing hypnosis. Suggestions made in the context in which the sympathetic nervous system is very active we shall label as *negative hypnosis*.

On the other hand, the Nancy School followed the procedures laid down by Braid. His method involved quiet repose, slow breathing and generally an activation of the parasympathetic nervous system. When the parasympathetic nervous system is activated it is also the case that the conscious mind is bypassed. As the parasympathetic nervous system becomes more activated so there is less need for the brain to bring into action the cortex – and it is an active cortex which inhibits hypnotic induction. When suggestions are made in the context of an activated parasympathetic nervous system, we shall label this as *positive hypnosis*.

The distinction between positive and negative hypnosis explains to a large extent the difference between some stage hypnosis and hypnosis used in hypnotherapy. Consider the following stage performance. A subject (victim!) is asked to stand stiffly to attention with their eyes closed. The stage hypnotist then makes a loud noise and sways the subject backwards laying them on the floor. The combination of eyes closed, loud noise and sudden movement in an unusual direction brings the sympathetic nervous system very quickly into action – and remember that the sympathetic system operates on various organs simultaneously. In such a state, suggestions made by the hypnotist are more readily accepted. The same negative kind of hypnosis is brought about by pressing on certain nerves and arteries. It is almost certainly the case that hypnosis induced in primitive tribal rituals (in the past and today) is also negative hypnosis. The person interested in self-hypnosis, and the hypnotherapist, is not concerned about inducing such negative hypnosis. Therapy and behaviour changes brought about by one's own suggestions can only be effective if the suggestions are made when the parasympathetic nervous system is active.

Notice finally, that whether positive or negative hypnosis is induced, the suggestions made may be the same and the response to them may be the same but the context in which they are made is quite different: in one it is with an active sympathetic nervous system, while in the other it is with an active parasympathetic nervous system.

The Brain

In this section we shall discuss three aspects of the brain: (1) its lateral structure, composed of three parts labelled the core brain, the limbic system and the cerebrum; (2) its vertical division into the right and left hemispheres; and (3) the electrical activity of the brain and the nature of different brainwave patterns. All three aspects have a bearing on the hypnotic state (and on many other forms of altered states of consciousness).

(1) THE STRUCTURE OF THE BRAIN

The lateral structure of the brain in terms of the core brain, the limbic system and the cerebrum is illustrated in Figure 2.

(a) The Core Brain

The *core brain* is the enlarged section of the spinal cord at the entry to the cranium. It is the most primitive evolutionarily of the three brain structures and is very much concerned with reflex actions – such as breathing, heart-rate, etc. The medulla oblongata controls breathing and some of the reflexes required to control posture. Slightly above the medulla oblongata and to the rear is the cerebellum, a rather convoluted structure which is important in co-ordinating movement and adjusting movement according to the environment. Movements once learned appear to get programmed into the cerebellum and then become automatic *without any conscious involvement*, such as picking something up, walking, writing, and so on. You may be consciously thinking about what you intend to write, but not about how to write! Thus, with practice, many learned actions can become quite automatic, e.g. driving, dancing, skating and typing. Above these two structures there is the *thalamus*. This appears to have two separate functions. One is to process and relay information to the cerebellum arising from sense receptors. The other is to mediate between the

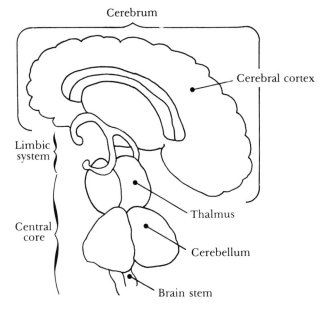

(a) Three layers of the brain

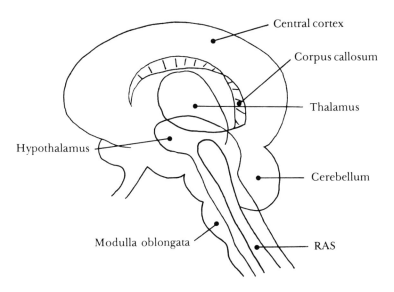

(b) Cross-section of the brain

Figure 2

reticular activating system and the cortex. In simple terms, it deals with the degree to which the cortex is activated, hence controlling sleep and wakefulness. The *hypothalamus*, much smaller than the thalamus and lying below it, is a very complex structure and seems to have a great many functions. It has an important role in motivation and emotion, it is involved in eating, drinking, sexual behaviour, sleeping, temperature control, homoeostasis (body equilibrium) and it regulates endocrine activity. In simple terms, it acts as a control mechanism. When the body becomes over-active or the emotions become aroused, it is the hypothalamus which re-establishes the body's equilibrium (homoeostasis).

One structure running through and between a number of the structures we have so far discussed is the *reticular activating system* (RAS). The RAS acts like an alarm clock and awakens the cortex so that it can interpret the incoming sensory signals. But unlike an alarm clock, it can also change as a result of signals from the cortex. This results in two pathways of nerves: one ascending and one descending. It would appear that the RAS determines what signals should reach the cortex, or even if any should reach the cortex. It obviously has an important bearing on what we understand by the term 'consciousness' or even 'being conscious'. A damaged RAS can lead to a permanent coma: to total lack of consciousness. Furthermore, the RAS plays a role in attention. When you are concentrating very hard on something you may not hear someone speaking to you. In this case, the signals from the ear have reached the RAS but this structure has not allowed them to penetrate to the cortex: you therefore do not consciously hear the person speaking to you. (You will hear the person unconsciously in the sense that the information is there in the RAS, and if it so wishes it can make the information available to the cortex. The signal as such cannot evaporate into nothing. It is simply a question of where in the nervous system the information is stored, and what other parts of the nervous system can have access to this information.) It is not an unreasonable conjecture that the RAS has an important role in establishing positive hypnosis.

(b) The Limbic System

The *limbic system* is a very complex group of structures around the central core of the brain which evolved later than the core brain. Early studies (around 1933) suggested that this structure activates the cortex in a non-specific way and that it was involved in emotional arousal. A major structure belonging to the limbic system is the hippocampus, which we shall discuss later, which has significant effects on behaviour. As we have already mentioned, the hypothalamus also has an important role and this too is part of the limbic system (indicating no clear demarcation between the three parts we are discussing). As more research has revealed, each element in the limbic system has a particular function.

This system is known to be where the brain 'decides' whether a sensation is one of pleasure or one of pain (also called reward and punishment), and is intimately connected with aggressive or non-aggressive behaviour and with motivation. It has been found (at least in animal experiments) that a sensory experience that leads to neither reward nor punishment is very soon forgotten. One important observation, at least for hypnosis, is that novel or new sensory input leads the limbic system to activate the cortex; while repetition of a stimulus over a period of time, which excites neither the reward nor the punishment centres, leads to no such activation of the cortex, what is referred to as *habituation*. On the other hand, if the stimulus causes either reward or punishment then the continued stimulus leads to more and more activation of the cortex. In other words, the response is *reinforced*.

The brain's response to a new or novel sensory input is called the *orienting reflex*, (see Luria[26]). It is the orienting reflex which allows you to become alert and attentive to the new or novel situation. When habituation occurs then the orienting reflex is not activated. But what undertakes the comparison in order to 'decide' that the stimulus is not novel or new and what blocks the orienting reflex? It is here that the hippocampus plays a role, and for the moment we shall simply say that in these circumstances the orienting reflex is replaced by a *conditioned reflex*. Luria makes the following important statement:

> Much human activity is evoked by intentions and plans, by forecasts and programmes which are formed during man's conscious life, which are social in their motivation and are effected with the close participation, initially of his external, and later of his internal *speech*. Every intention formulated in speech defines a certain goal and evokes a programme of action leading to the attainment of that goal. Every time the goal is reached activity

stops, but every time it is not reached, this leads to further mobilization of efforts. (p.57)[26]

The mechanisms that largely bring this about belong to the limbic system of the brain and its relationship with the core brain and the cortex.

(c) The Cerebrum

Covering the core brain and limbic system is the *cerebrum*, the largest part of which is the cerebral cortex, the most recently evolved section of the brain and the most highly developed in man. It is in the cortex that complex mental activities take place. The cortex is itself divided into two hemispheres, separated by a collection of nerves called the corpus callosum. We shall deal with both of these later. Quite a bit is known about the functional activity of various parts of the cortex as they effect movement, body-sense area, sight, hearing and language. There are also what are called *associated areas* which are not so specific in function and are concerned with learning, memory and thinking. Important as this research is, it is not that germane to our present study, for the basic reason that hypnosis is attempting to 'switch-off' such cortical activity.

However, this research does indicate that the cerebral cortex is able to block synaptic connections and so prevent the flow of information into conscious awareness. Eccles, in particular, has been concerned with these developments and makes the following point about synaptic inhibition in relation to hypnosis and meditation.

> Thus we can account for the afferent anaesthesias of hypnosis or of yoga or of acupuncture by the cerebral and other pathways to the brain. In all these cases discharges from the cerebral cortex down the pyramidal tract and other pathways will exert an inhibitory blockage at the relays in the spinocortical pathways. (pp. 254-5).[35]

This views the brain not in terms of 'windows' of the mind, but rather as a means of discarding irrelevant information.

(2) THE DIVIDED BRAIN

The cerebral cortex is divided vertically into two halves, called the left and right hemispheres. Although they appear as symmetrical structures modern research has shown that there is a difference in function.[5, 38, 44] The functional differences between the two halves have a great deal to do with a person's psychological functions, although not only these.

The left hemisphere of the brain controls the right side of the body while the right hemisphere controls the left side of the body. More important from our present point of view is the type of function each hemisphere is responsible for. Although there are no hard and fast rules, in general, there is a pattern of specialization which is fairly common. This is indicated in Figure 3.

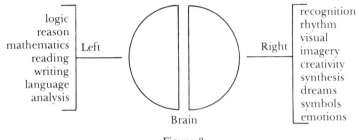

Figure 3

It is clear from Figure 3 that what we commonly think of as 'conscious thought' takes place largely (although not wholly) in the left hemisphere; while many functions we commonly think of as 'unconscious thought' take place largely (although not wholly) in the right hemisphere.

The simplest way of thinking about the specialization of the brain is to consider the brain's process while you are talking to someone. Your left brain is picking up what they are saying and processing the information and then activating your speech centres for your reply. *At the same time*, your right brain is considering the other person's facial expressions, their mannerisms, the intonation in their voice, etc. In other words, the left brain is processing verbal cues while the right brain is processing non-verbal cues. Now if the two halves could not communicate with one another this would not be a sensible procedure. But information taken in by one hemisphere is passed to the other by means of the corpus callosum, with which we shall deal in more detail later. The verbal and non-verbal incoming information can either be in agreement or can be conflicting. ('A person might not mean what they say' can be interpreted here as their non-verbal cues indicating a different response from their verbal cues.) It is vital for the hypnotherapist to realize this. Rapport, which we discussed briefly in Chapter 1, depends not only on verbal communication but also on non-verbal responses. Furthermore, the induction procedures that are available also involve, to different degrees, non-verbal suggestions. A hypnotist may be unsuccessful in hypnotizing someone, not because of their verbal technique, but rather because they are giving out non-verbal cues to which the subject does not wish to respond.

For the autohypnotist, knowledge of the hemispherical specialization of the brain gives him or her insight into the hypnotic state itself. The induction procedure, whether self-induced or induced by someone else, activates the para-sympathetic nervous system. We said earlier that this would lead to a reduction in activity of the cortex. But this is only partially correct. The left hemisphere of the cortex is what is being reduced in activity because the induction procedure does not require logical reasoning. However, this is not necessarily true of the right hemisphere of the brain. A number of the suggestions involve imagery, such as being warm and comfortable while lying on a beach. Such images are specifically directed at activating the right hemisphere of the brain where such imagery is largely (although not wholly) processed. If the induction procedure is successful then the left hemisphere will not check this information against reality – that is, no reality-testing will take place. If no reality-testing takes place, then as far as the nervous system is concerned this information is correct and the body will accordingly respond to it.

The process just described is not simply a question of hemispherical specialization. We have made the point that the brain is composed of three interrelated structures. All three structures are probably involved in this procedure. For instance, the induction procedure, by involving repetitive phrases, leads to habituation which is part of the limbic system. The conjecture being advanced here is that hypnosis involves a particular relationship being established, between the various parts of the brain, which is sufficiently distinct from other configurations, such as being awake or being asleep.

The research on split-brain patients has led Eccles[9] to conclude that consciousness resides in the left hemisphere of the brain. The basis for this conclusion is that if the two hemispheres are separated by cutting the corpus callosum (which has been done in some extreme cases of epilepsy) then experiences which are picked up *only* by the right hemisphere of the brain will not be transmitted to the left hemisphere. As far as the individual is concerned they will not be consciously aware of them. There is no way that they can communicate such awareness through speech. However, they can still respond unconsciously by non-verbal means, but in this case they cannot consciously account for their actions!

Interest in the connection between hemispherical specialization of the brain and hypnosis has led to some interesting studies. One is that undertaken at London's Charing Cross Hospital Medical School under Dr John Gruzelier of the psychiatry department.[32] In this research they have been studying people's electrical skin conductance during hypnotic induction. Electrodermal response is generally considered an indication of how much attention a person is paying to a particular stimulus or stimuli. The experiment involved running a hypnotic induction tape for seven minutes during which time subjects were also played a number of one-second seventy decibel tones at regular intervals. Dr Gruzelier explains the basis of his approach as follows,

> . . . to achieve effective induction, one has to narrow one's attention to what the hypnotist is saying and a susceptible subject will be the person who can best focus his attention initially.

The aim of the tones, therefore, is to distract the individual from concentrating on the hypnotic induction tape. The article continues,

> Before induction, the people who subsequently proved susceptible to hypnosis had greater electrodermal responses in their left than in their right hand. The opposite was true of unsusceptible individuals. As the induction tape was played, this asymmetry was reversed in susceptible people, the right hand responses becoming the larger. But no such effect was seen when unsusceptible subjects were played the same induction tape.
>
> Because of the known associations between electrodermal activity and brain hemispheres, it seems that susceptible individuals start off with the left side of their brain holding sway and then, under induction, switch over to the right side. The susceptible people also habituated faster to the intrusive tones – they showed fewer electrodermal responses – suggesting they were able to ignore them.

The hypnotic state seems to be associated with the right hemisphere of the brain [according to Dr Gruzelier and his team]; its dream-like quality, altered time sense, attitude of passive acceptance and several other characteristics all suggest this. And under hypnosis this was confirmed in that the susceptible subjects did switch into a right hemisphere 'mode'.

Dr Gruzelier points out that what matters is the *left*-brain dominance of those who are susceptible but who can switch to right-brain dominance during the hypnosis. The left-brain dominance during induction is important in order for the individual to 'focus his attention'. Unsusceptible subjects, however, start with right-brain dominance, with its associated 'broadened attention' such that they cannot concentrate sufficiently on the induction even to begin to be hypnotized.

Studies, such as this, shed considerable light on the hypnotic process. It also suggests that a simple statement that hypnosis is all to do with the right brain may be incorrect.

(3) BRAINWAVES

The brain is an electro-chemical structure and as such it gives off an electrical charge which can be measured. An electro-encephalogram (EEG) is a tracing of the changes in the voltage of the brain over time. It must always be remembered that the EEG is a composite of all the millions of nerves cells which are firing in the brain. With such diversity of activity it might be thought that the brain would show no obvious pattern – that the EEG would indicate asynchronous activity. For the awake and alert person this is largely the case. However, under certain conditions the brain cells achieve synchronous activity and in such circumstances wave patterns emerge which are observable on the EEG.

Table 2

Brainwave Patterns

Wave	Frequency Cycles per second	Typical situations of occurrence
Alpha	8-12	Awake and quietly resting, meditation, hypnosis
Beta	14-50	Normal waking alertness
Theta	4-7	Emotional stress, deep meditation
Delta	less than 3½	Deep sleep, infants

Different waves have been discerned and are classified as to their frequency per second (where the frequency of a wave is measured as the number of cycles: a cycle consisting of the curve from one high point to the next high point). Table 2 gives the four waves discussed in the literature: the alpha, beta, theta and delta waves.

The normal awake and alert person exhibits largely beta waves, which denote effectively an unsynchronized pattern since the range of frequencies is quite large (and can reach up to fifty cycles per second). But even in this state it is possible to have short bursts of alpha waves. While some people can have varying degrees of alpha waves others show very little indeed.

It is now well documented that alpha is more likely to occur when a person is resting with their eyes closed and engaged in very little (conscious) mental activity – a very significant observation for hypnosis and meditation. The paradox of alpha is that it decreases both with drowsiness and with difficult mental tasks. Hypnosis, like meditation in this respect, is aimed at achieving alpha without going into drowsiness and not activating conscious mental processes. That hypnosis and sleep are quite different can be discerned from EEG patterns of sleep as compared with those of hypnosis. The EEG pattern of sleep has been more thoroughly investigated and we shall not discuss it here. Suffice it to say that sleep is considered to be composed of four stages which go through various wave patterns, only part of which are similar to hypnosis – namely, the period when alpha predominates at stage 1. In fact this is often referred to as a hypnopompic state. But as F. J. Evans rightly points out[11]:

> The available evidence suggests that there is no similarity between hypnosis and sleep in the EEG, although without independent criteria of both hypnosis and the relevant sleep stage, any hypothesized similarity is difficult to evaluate conclusively. (p. 53)

As Table 2 indicates, the EEG pattern found during hypnosis is predominantly (but not wholly) that of alpha. More significant for the autohypnotist is the now commonly held view that alpha can be brought under conscious control; that is to say, a person can learn to generate alpha waves. One should not fall into the trap, however, of assuming – because alpha waves occur during hypnosis – that one is the cause of the other. But it is a fair conjecture that those individuals who generate little alpha, or who find it difficult to achieve alpha waves by biofeedback methods (see Chapter 7), will also find autohypnosis difficult. Evans, however, found no correlation between alpha activity and hypnotizability, although the studies he cites did not involve sophisticated instrumentation which would be required in a proper analysis.

One final observation about brainwaves, important for hypnosis, is worth making. Early studies of brainwaves showed that there is an alpha blocking response. If an individual is in a restful state, with their eyes closed and not engaging in complex mental activity, then such a person will exhibit alpha waves on the EEG. If, however, they open their eyes then the alpha pattern no longer occurs: there has been a blocking of the alpha pattern. When the eyes are once again closed then alpha returns. We have not the space to discuss this in detail,[7, 46] but it does indicate why closing the eyes is so important in achieving and deepening the hypnotic state. It appears to be connected with the role of the hippocampus and the process of attention, conditioning and habituation. More significantly for the autohypnotist is the view now held that alpha can be achieved by conscious means. With practice and conditioning this does mean that the alpha wave pattern can also be maintained when the eyes are open. This has certainly been shown to be the case with practised Zen meditators.

Some Important Structures of the Brain

In this final section we shall discuss three rather complex structures in the brain in more detail: the corpus callosum; the thalamus, along with the hypothalamus; and the hippocampus. All three (or four since the hypothalamus is quite distinct from the thalamus) have been more thoroughly investigated in recent years. Our purpose, then, is to outline briefly these researches and speculate on what implications they may have for hypnosis, and especially autohypnosis.

(1) THE CORPUS CALLOSUM

The *corpus callosum* is a large bundle of nerve fibres dividing, yet connecting, the two hemispheres of the cortex. It is, in fact, the largest fibre bundle in the brain and because of this it was thought to have an important function in relation to the two hemispheres of the brain. Yet until the 1960s its function was a complete mystery. It was a complete mystery in the sense that when it was cut nothing in the brain appeared to be affected by such an operation – nothing at least in terms of the standard psychological tests. Furthermore, attention was not focused on the right-left characteristics of the brain because lesions in the right hemisphere did not appear to have any great debilitating effect. Better experimental design, however, revealed quite major differences between the two hemispheres as we pointed out above, and summarized in Figure 3.

The corpus callosum relays information between the two hemispheres. Information that is picked up by one hemisphere is quickly relayed to the other and combined with related information taken in by that hemisphere and vice versa. The corpus callosum acts like a huge cable between two computer banks, each computer receiving different information about the same phenomenon. So long as the cable is operating, information flows between the two computers and a more complete view of the phenomenon is established. In terms of the brain, this implies a single consciousness: a single and integrated view of the outside world. It is also believed, although this has not yet been established, that the corpus callosum helps in reconciling conflicting sensory information received by the two hemispheres. Furthermore, the structure does have a bearing on the brain establishing a synchronized wave pattern. (In the case of the epileptic, cutting the corpus callosum prevents the whole brain synchronizing and so it lessens the extent of an attack.)

We know that the right hemisphere controls the left side of the body and the left hemisphere the right side of the body. Consider now a decision to pick up a cup. You can do this with either hand. You do not find yourself first putting out one hand, then pulling it back to use the other, or in a state of complete indecision. One hand reaches out and picks up the cup. This implies that one hemisphere has taken dominance in carrying out this particular act. But this further implies that the other hemisphere must have been inhibited from carrying out the same act. It would appear that this is a function of the corpus callosum. For any act only one hemisphere is dominant. Which hemisphere is dominant depends not only on the corpus callosum but also on information from the limbic system which 'alerts' the appropriate hemisphere.

The conclusion we come to is that at any one time conscious control is given to only one hemisphere. One feature of hypnotic induction is to ensure that conscious control is given to the right hemisphere of the brain. By closing the eyes and reducing sensory input, and also by means of suggestion, the 'alert' mechanism is not activating the left hemisphere and it would appear, although this is only conjecture, that less information traverses the corpus callosum. When this is achieved, as it is in hypnosis and other altered states of consciousness, the nervous system responds to the suggestions as if they are true. Why? Because it is the left hemisphere which is involved in reality-testing, and since this is temporarily in abeyance, then no reality-testing takes place. The person accordingly responds as if the information were true.

(2) THE THALAMUS AND HYPOTHALAMUS

The *thalamus* is important because it acts like a relay station between the incoming sensory input of sight, sound and touch (but not smell) and the cortex of the brain. The thalamus not only interprets what the signal means, but it also 'decides' whether it is pleasant or unpleasant (reward or punishment). The thalamus also processes information from the cerebellum and other parts of the limbic system, and for this reason also plays a part in motor control (e.g., body posture) and emotion.

The thalamus, besides processing information, is also vital in maintaining consciousness, alertness and attention. In this process it works along with the cortex and the reticular activating system. It is as if the reticular formation along with the thalamus 'turns on' or 'turns off' the cortex. (It is also more appropriate to think of only part of the cortex being turned off or turned on, and not the cortex as a whole.)

Beneath the thalamus is the much smaller structure, the *hypothalamus*. This structure controls the body's short-run and long-run equilibrium: its homoeostasis. To do this it controls both nerve responses and endocrine responses by changing electrical signals and changing hormonal balance. It affects the whole body both in the short run and in the long run. Of course other parts of the brain are passing to it relevant information necessary for such control.

From the point of view of hypnosis, the hypothalamus can be influenced by messages from the cortex. As we have already pointed out, if hypnosis is achieved and the right brain is dominant, then no reality-testing takes place. If a hypnotist now suggests that the person is in a desert and it is very hot and that they are very thirsty and have not had any water for some time, then it is the hypothalamus which will begin to send out signals to various parts of the body. The person will feel thirsty because liquid is required to re-establish equilibrium in such an environment. The fact that the person is not in such an environment is irrelevant to the workings of the hypothalamus: it simply acts on the information which it receives.

(3) THE HIPPOCAMPUS

The *hippocampus* is one of the most paradoxical brain structures. More is known about its structure than virtually any other part of the limbic system but still very little is known about its function! What is known is that it has something to do with the recognition of novelty, with learning and with memory. Our only concern here is with its recognition of novelty. When something is novel then you pay it attention until it becomes familiar. Once the familiarity is achieved then attention can be switched off or re-directed. The hippocampus appears, then, to be a source of decision-making, and can lead to inhibition of inappropriate behaviour.

The habituation response has been analysed particularly by the Russian Sokolov. With the aid of the hippocampus, a stimulus when first encountered is compared with information already stored in the brain. If it considers the stimulus novel then the orienting reflex is activated and the person pays particular attention to it. If it is not novel then the orienting reflex is not activated.

It is this feature which is attempted in the induction process of (positive) hypnosis. It may also account for why some people find it difficult to enter hypnosis. If the person pays attention to what the hypnotist is doing then the orienting reflex is highly likely to be operative. In this case the person finds it difficult 'to let go'. The point is that if this conjecture is correct then while the orienting reflex is operative the hippo-campus, in conjunction with the reticular activating system, will continue to activate parts of the left cortical hemisphere. For the autohypnotist there is also a lesson to learn from this analysis. Continued practice will soon stop the orienting reflex from being activated. The hippocampus at some point decides the whole process has been heard before and so pays it no particular attention. With practice a person can enter hypnosis quickly because the orienting reflex no longer occurs when induction takes place. The simple message, of course, is not to pay attention to the hypnotic induction – even when being induced by yourself.

Conclusion
Although this chapter has contained some rather technical material it is hoped that it provides a more reasoned basis for hypnosis. Although during hypnosis as such you should not consider what is taking place, this does not of course mean that you should not do so in your normal waking state. As more information becomes available on the workings of the brain there is no doubt that a number of the conjectures made in this chapter will need to be revised.

3.
Consciousness and Altered States of Consciousness

In order to come to some understanding of altered states of consciousness (ASC), let us begin with an analogy. Consider three light bulbs which we have labelled A, B and C in Table 3. Now at any one time we can have a different possible situation (a different state of illumination) depending on whether different lights are on or off. There are, in fact, eight possible states shown in Table 3.

Table 3

States	A	Lights B	C
1	on	on	on
2	on	on	off
3	on	off	off
4	off	on	on
5	on	off	on
6	off	on	off
7	off	off	on
8	off	off	off

(In fact with n lights there are 2^n possible states.) Suppose we now define something to be so only when light A is on. Then this definition is satisfied in a total of four different states (1,2,3 and 5). If, on the other hand, we define something as requiring both lights A and B to be on, then we have only two states which satisfy this condition (1 and 2).

If we push the analogy to an extreme we can think of state 1 as being conscious and state 8 as being asleep. But between these two extremes there are six other possible states each different from both 1 and 8 in at least one respect. These other six states (along with 8) can be likened to altered states of consciousness. The analogy is quite useful in this respect. It indicates, as is the case, that there is not *one* altered state of consciousness but many. For instance, state 3 may arise under LSD while state 7 may occur under mystical experiences. Although, as we have said, this is pushing the analogy to extremes, it does make the important point that the brain passes through many states both during the day and over the maturation of the nervous system. Some states occur once during a twenty-four hour cycle, such as 1 and 8 (consciousness and sleep) while others, like mystical states, may never occur in a person's lifespan. The difficulty faced is in identifying the different states and establishing under what conditions they occur. One of these states is the hypnotic state. The difficulty is in distinguishing it from other states.

The analogy, although useful up to a point, has a major shortcoming. Although it is true that nerves act like lights in that they either fire (the light is on) or do not (the light is off), what is probably more important is that the brain has a number of electrical cycles. These cycles are distinguished by waves: called alpha, beta, delta and theta waves, as highlighted in Table 2 (p.36). To get some idea of what this means let us return to our analogy. Suppose all the lights went on and off at random. Then we would observe no cycle: we would over twenty-four hours show constant changing patterns, possibly being awake one moment (state 1) and asleep the next (state 8). We know this is not true. Suppose, however, that the lights have a sequence such that A, B and C are on for sixteen hours and are off for seven hours thirty minutes, and that this sequence is the same every twenty-four hours. For the remaining thirty minutes the lights pass from state 1 into state 8 at random (with, say, the exception of state 7 – the mystical state). Now if we looked at the brain in state 1 we could discern its electrical state, which is characterized by lights A, B and C being on. Similarly we could discern the electrical state of the brain in state 8, characterized by no lights being on (but where we are assuming some electrical potential can be measured). The electrical pattern in each case also shows a cycle with amplitude and wave length. Consciousness, state 1, is characterized by a beta cycle; while sleep, state 8, is characterized by a delta cycle. Although in practice all waves are likely to be present in any state, one or two will predominate. The strongest cycle at any moment of time will govern the observed state of the individual. This is important. Even while conscious, and so characterized by beta waves, it is possible to measure some alpha waves – but these are swamped by beta waves. Furthermore, some waves are under conscious control while others, like alpha waves, can only be brought under conscious control with training.

With this analogy in mind, what have writers said about altered states of consciousness, ASC? Tart admitted, in 1969,[45] that at the present time we really do not know precisely what it is. He was content to state that a person's 'normal' state of consciousness is the one in which he spends the major part of his waking hours'; while 'An altered state of consciousness for a given individual is one in which he clearly feels a *qualitative* shift in his pattern of mental functioning.' He leaves the volume itself to clarify the point. Ludwig[25] gives a useful working definition:

> An altered state(s) of consciousness [is] any mental state(s) induced by various physiological, psychological, or pharmacological manoeuvres or agents, which can be recognized subjectively by the individual himself (or by an objective observer of the individual) as representing a sufficient deviation in subjective experience or psychological functioning from certain general norms for that individual during alert, waking consciousness.

But this is no more than an elaborate version of Tart's more straightforward statement.

The difficulty in distinguishing different states of mind, different states of consciousness, is exemplified in trying to distinguish autosuggestion from autohypnosis. Are these states of mind the same or different? First we must recognize that suggestion is a force. Baudouin[3] comes to this idea when he says that suggestion involves an idea which undergoes transformation into action. If the idea is given by the person themselves then this constitutes autosuggestion; while if it is given by another person then this constitutes heterosuggestion. But as Baudouin emphasizes, what is important is the transformation into action. *The transformation into action is what constitutes the force.* Furthermore, this transformation takes place at the unconscious level.

But having stated that autosuggestion is an unconscious transformation of an idea into action, how does it differ from autohypnosis? I may walk along the street and give myself a suggestion to feel cheerful and this idea may take root at the unconscious level, but this is autosuggestion and not autohypnosis. The difference lies in the *context* in which the suggestion is given. In other words, the difference lies in the frame of mind the individual is in when the suggestion is made. For instance, if I first get into a relaxed state and then make a suggestion to myself that when I walk along the street I will feel cheerful, then this is autohypnosis. The suggestion is the same as before, but the context in which it was made is different. But the context is not simply a relaxed state: it is more than this. It is also a *receptive* state. The autosuggestion may or may not take root in the unconscious mind. In autohypnosis the context *deliberately* creates the right environment so that suggestions can take root and there is a greater probability for them to take root. It does not mean, of course, that the autohypnotic suggestions will automatically take root, only that there is an increased probability that they will do so.

The conclusion that we draw from this discussion is that autosuggestions occur during normal waking consciousness, while autohypnosis involves suggestions made in an altered state of consciousness. In other words, the suggestions made may be the same but the state of consciousness is different.

There is little disagreement in the literature that hypnosis is one particular ASC -- with the possible exception of Barber.[2] He, however, is confusing the issue. His main contention is that nearly all (or even all) of the phenomena which can be produced in hypnosis can be produced in normal waking consciousness. But he is defining things not in terms of the context but rather in terms of what things can be done in that context. The point is that the context allows the *same* things to be done in a qualitatively, and often quantitatively, different way. By concentrating on the phenomenon Barber is simply confusing the issue. I can do everything (or almost everything) awake that I can do while asleep, but I would not therefore say that sleep does not exist!

The main difficulty investigators have is in trying to distinguish hypnosis as one particular ASC from other ASCs, e.g. meditation. The confusion is compounded when we note that a number of drugs can create similar features which are characteristic of hypnosis – such as time distortion. But all this points out is our limited knowledge at the present moment of time. Suppose, to return to our analogy of light bulbs, that we knew enough to distinguish all eight states. Let us further suppose that time distortion occurs when light B is off. Then four altered states of consciousness involve time distortion (states 3,5,7 and 8). Even now we know that drug states, hypnosis and sleep involve time distortion. (Even waking consciousness does to a very small degree.) At the present time research is investigating the light bulbs – as to whether they are on or off – but not yet the states, since we lack enough information.

Even sleep, which is also an ASC, has only fairly recently been investigated in any depth. But the more we investigate, the more the problems mount up. We know, for instance, that the sleep state has three phases. Are these also ASCs or simply small deviations from the state we classify as sleep? In Ludwig's definition there had to be a significant deviation from certain general norms. The same could be said of sleep. The three phases, although distinguishable, are not sufficiently deviating from the norms of sleep to be a different ASC. At the same time the hypnotic state *is* significantly different from both normal waking consciousness and from sleep to be worth considering separately.

It is only when our attention is focused on ASC that we require to distinguish degrees. It is now common to point out that in most countries people simply talk of 'snow', not shades, types or whatever: simply 'snow'. Icelanders are known, however, to talk of many different types. The different types have different characteristics which are *important for them*. In Britain it was once common to talk of hard and soft water – and it still is. But now we also distinguish chlorinated from unchlorinated water. The point is that 'water' has a whole range: from pure distilled water to whole varieties of polluted water. We have for too long talked about 'consciousness' as if it were a *single* state. Freud, more than anyone else, raised the importance of the unconscious (or subconscious). But still there was simply the two: conscious mind and subconscious mind. It is time we recognized many states of mind, different ASCs. Only when we become interested in them will we begin to discern the many varieties there are. Hypnosis is just one of the variety of ASCs that are now being recognized.

The difficulty of distinguishing the state is nicely illustrated by Huxley's state of *deep reflection* (his own term for his altered state of consciousness). This, in my view, is no more than self-hypnosis. This is denied by Huxley and by Erickson, who undertook the experiment with Huxley. Any person engaging in self-hypnosis would benefit from reading Erickson's account of Huxley's experiences, which is reported in Tart.[45]

Development of Human Consciousness

We concluded the previous section by saying that 'consciousness' was not a single state. But we can go further. Not only is it not a single state, neither is it a thing or repository. This important point is made in Jaynes' book on the bicameral mind,[23] where he states, '[Consciousness] is an operator rather than a thing or repository. And it is intimately bound up with volition and decision.' (p.55) An *operator* acts on something and is not itself an entity. In justifying this conclusion, Jaynes looks into the development of human consciousness. He argues that consciousness came after language. In support of this contention he considers the Homeric legends (the *Iliad* and the *Odyssey*) from a psychological point of view. When this is done the most striking thing is that they contain *no* mental acts. There is no distinction between the soma and the psyche: no distinction between body and mind. They contain action and instructions from the gods. In his view, the gods take the place of what we now call consciousness. In this bicameral mind,

> volition came as a voice that was in the nature of a neurological command, in which the command and the action were separated, in which to hear was to obey. (p.99)[23]

A number of people have experienced 'voices in their head', not their own voice, but voices just as real (or even more real?) than if someone were speaking to them. What is clear is that such voices occur either in times of relaxation or in times of emotional stress. In the time of Homer, such voices were common. To show that this is not historical sophistry, but rather a feature of the human nervous system, all we need to do is turn to the studies on schizophrenia. In this state hallucinations abound – and the auditory more frequently than the visual. As with the heroes of the *Odyssey* and the *Iliad*, so the schizophrenic invariably finds he must obey his auditory instructions.

The question which comes out of this brief discussion is: at what point did volition, will and conscious decision-making manifest themselves in the development of man? Jaynes would argue that it is a very recent development. Such a development is linked with the increased size of the brain and especially the frontal lobes. This can be established (or at least has been established) by brain seizures and various lobotomies. The outcome of these for individuals has been difficulties in making decisions, formulating plans and generally engaging in purposeful activities. In addition, consciousness is very much left-brain dominated. This domination, however, only arises from the fact that most of the logical and linguistic faculties (but not all) are contained in the left hemisphere of the brain. However, such hemispherical distinction is inadequate to account for human consciousness. We have already pointed out in Chapter 2 that the brain has three interrelated parts. These interrelate more in a lateral than a horizontal fashion. To say that human consciousness is a function simply of the left hemisphere is almost certainly wrong; that the left hemisphere plays a significant role in human consciousness is almost certainly correct.

The connection between hemispherical specialization and consciousness has, for example, led Ornstein[33] to argue that people have two modes of consciousness: one linear and rational, the other arational and intuitive. The former is associated with the left hemisphere of the brain, while the latter is associated with the right hemisphere. He goes on to say,

> If we can realize, from the outset, that our ordinary consciousness is something we must of necessity construct or *create* in order to survive in the world, then we can understand that this consciousness is only *one* possible consciousness. And if this consciousness is a *personal* construction, then each person can change his consciousness simply by *changing the way* he constructs it. (pp.33-4)[33]

Of course, this is not the only view of consciousness. Two broad views arise in the vast literature on this topic. First, consciousness is generated by brain activity but plays no causal role in people's behaviour; it is a by-product – just like heat is a by-product of combustion. This is referred to as the *epiphenomenalist* view. A second view is that consciousness is generated by brain activity, but can influence brain mechanisms and, in turn, behaviour. This is referred to as the *interactionist* view. As will become clear in this book, the present author leans very much towards interactionism.

Why, it may be asked, have we discussed human consciousness when our interest is with hypnosis, and, especially, autohypnosis? The point being made is that only recently have we considered in any depth the phenomenon of consciousness. Freud broke totally new ground when he went even further to consider the subconscious. The studies into sleep, drugs, meditation – along with hypnosis – have all added to our knowledge of the mind, its various states and (some of) its dynamic properties. Hypnosis cannot be considered in isolation. It is just one altered state of consciousness. The question that we wish to raise is whether hypnosis is a retrogressive step into an earlier state of mind. Put in a totally different way: was it easier to hypnotize people say, in the time of Homer, than it is now? If so, what has changed?

These are almost impossible questions to answer because the people of Homer's day are not here now. We can only consider the literature of the Bible, the documents of Egypt and the sleep temples of Greece. At the same time we can consider other cultures less developed than our own. Here, hypnotic trance states again appear more common. What we need to separate is the unscientific, inaccurate, prejudicial and even fanatical statements from the hard core. We have already noted in our history of hypnosis how Mesmer believed in magnetic forces. Although 'scientific' (at least in its day) it was false. Not only that but the general belief, both then and to some extent now, that the hypnotist has some power over the hypnotized person gives to the hypnotic state something which is totally unnecessary. In autohypnosis no such power exists. The reason is that it never did exist – except in people's imagination. What the Nancy school demonstrated was the importance of suggestion. But they too concentrated on too narrow a range. Even Baudouin overstated the scientific nature of the subject. He stated that the effect of a suggestion is the square of the emotional involvement. Although it is true that the emotional involvement plays a most important role, this particular 'law' is simply a restatement of Kepler's second law of planetary motions. Baudouin is overstating the case and is trying to make 'scientific' what, given our present state of knowledge, cannot be stated so precisely.

What we need is to discuss hypnosis as an ASC. In doing this we must try to distinguish it from other ASCs and also recognize that it is a subjective state. When we look back at the development of consciousness we see that that discussion is about various states of consciousness, where normal waking consciousness is but one of the states. Its importance lies in the fact that a person spends most of his time in such a state. It does not necessarily mean that it is the most important state. The mystic would argue that his mystical experience, sometimes just two minutes in duration, is the most significant and important thing in his life. Why? Because from then on his normal waking consciousness takes on a different meaning. But more significantly, nothing in normal waking consciousness can compare *qualitatively* with the brief mystical experience. We do not have to turn to mystical experiences either. Peak experiences (to use Maslow's term), insights etc., have similar qualities – but to a lesser degree. They are all brief and occur during ASCs.

We can, however, learn something from our discussion so far. *Consciousness is a barrier to the hypnotic state.* If we are in a normal waking conscious state then we cannot be in hypnosis. We must change the mental state; we must alter it. Now this can either be done by someone else, by drugs or by oneself. All three means are possible; and they are also possible in creating the hypnotic state. This should not be surprising. It is the state of mind which *is* hypnosis, not the means by which the state is brought about. We can talk of fire without confusing it with whether the fire was brought about by lighting a match or using a lighter. So we must constantly remember that hypnosis is a state of mind independent of how that state is achieved.

Can one consciously alter the normal waking state? This is a confusing question. The hypnotic state can be achieved only by *suspending consciousness*. In other words, we stop the *process* of consciousness, we put a halt to the *operator*. By suspending its operation we allow a change in consciousness from the normal to take place. This is *not* a retrogressive step. It does not mean that we are going into a more primitive form of consciousness. It simply means that we are going into *another* form of consciousness. The point can be made in the following way. Suppose I have a piano and play a Strauss waltz, is that retrogressive? It is true that it is music common in the early twentieth century but it is in no way inferior; it is just another kind of music. Just as a Strauss waltz is different from an Oscar Peterson jazz composition, so hypnosis is different from the normal conscious waking state.

We have laboured this point in an attempt to indicate that

ASCs are alternatives. One is no better than another or more primitive than another. Certainly many ASCs activate the lower limbic system of the brain. But that only reflects that consciousness is less associated with these areas of the brain. We are, in fact, no more than saying that the brain has areas of specialization. All efficient systems have areas and parts which are specialized. The human nervous system is one of the most (the most?) efficient systems we know – its efficiency far outstrips anything man-made.

The difficulty is that we do not know exactly what hypnosis is. We know a number of its characteristics but not exactly what it is. If we return to the analogy of the light bulbs, we know that certain lights should be on, and some off, but there are many others we do not know about. Some of these same lights are off or on in other ASCs also, but our knowledge does not extend across the whole range of lights and so we cannot distinguish the two states. This is the dilemma: our present state of knowledge does not allow us to clearly distinguish various ASCs. Tart ([45]p.235) goes as far as saying that hypnosis refers to a *range* of ASCs.

Definition of Hypnosis

Up to this point we have avoided trying to define hypnosis. We have argued that it is an altered state of consciousness; that it occurs when consciousness is suspended; that there can be positive or negative hypnotic states depending upon whether it is the parasympathetic or sympathetic nervous system which is being altered; and finally, that it is a subjective state.

Let us begin by noting five definitions of hypnosis:

(1) Hypnosis is a complex of two fundamental processes. The first is the construction of a special, temporary orientation to a small range of preoccupations and the second is the relative fading of the generalized reality-orientation into nonfunctional awareness. (Shor,[43]pp.249-50)

(2) Hypnosis is an altered state of the organism originally and usually produced by a repetition of stimuli in which suggestion (no matter how defined) is more effective than usual. (Marcuse,[29] p.21)

(3) Hypnosis is essentially a particular state of mind which is usually induced in one person by another. It is a state of mind

in which suggestions are not only more readily accepted than in the waking state, but are also acted upon much more powerfully than would be possible under normal conditions. (Hartland,[18] p.13)

(4) Hypnosis. Artificially-induced state, similar in some respects to sleep, but specially characterized by exaggerated *suggestibility*, and the continuance of contact or *rapport* with the operator. (*Penguin Dictionary of Psychology*).

(5) Hypnosis is an altered state of awareness effected by total concentration on the voice of the therapist. It will result in measurable physical, neurophysiological and psychological changes in which may be produced distortion of emotion, sensation, image and time.(Waxman,[49] p.43)

These definitions are quite diverse. They all to some extent capture the appropriate characteristics but they differ largely on which characteristics they consider as important. The characteristic which has had the least attention in the literature is the part of the nervous system which is being activated – the sympathetic (negative hypnosis) or the parasympathetic (positive hypnosis). Both positive and negative hypnosis satisfy, for example, Shor's construction of a special temporary orientation and a relative fading of the generalized reality-orientation, but each involves a different part of the nervous system. In so far as either the sympathetic or parasympathetic nervous system can be most active in a hypnotic state, *but not both*, then we may agree with Tart that more than one ASC is involved in hypnosis.

The reason for highlighting positive and negative hypnosis is not only that this has been neglected but also that it reveals that the early hypnotic states during the time of Mesmer and the Salpêtrière Institute, involving as they did hysterical and catatonic states, were almost wholly negative hypnotic states. When it was realized that suggestion played an important role, what went unnoticed was that suggestion largely operated on the parasympathetic nervous system. Today the common form of hypnosis is positive. More importantly for the autohypnotist, it is the positive form which is therapeutic. The fact that it activates the parasympathetic nervous system means that it reduces tension in the body – and this is irrespective of what other suggestions are made during the hypnotic state.

The observation that hypnosis is an activation of the parasympathetic nervous system helps to dispel some clearly incorrect notions about hypnosis. Helleberg[19] tries to make a distinction between meditation and hypnosis. She says,

> meditation is a state of restful *alertness*, of *heightened* awareness, while hypnosis tends to *suppress* awareness. (p.6)

This is not the case. Self-hypnosis, in this respect at least, also produces restful alertness, heightened awareness. Meditation and hypnosis have this in common. Even her comment on Christopher Isherwood (who says 'if it's [i.e., meditation] nothing but auto-hypnosis, you'll soon find out. Hypnosis wouldn't give you any lasting results.') is only partially true. Continued self-hypnosis with no particular suggestions will give you similar benefits to meditation. Why? Because both reduce anxiety and body tension – both stimulate the parasympathetic nervous system. The difference about lasting effects is that meditation can bring about a change in consciousness in terms of deeper understanding. But this is by no means peculiar to meditation. Some lasting changes can occur in hypnotherapy. But it is the case that these changes are a result of the therapy and not the hypnosis.

Submergence of the Self

In discussing White's *A Preface to a Theory of Hypnotism*,[50] Shor comments on his two features of hypnotism: (1) goal-directed striving and (2) an altered psychological state. Although (1) gained the most attention at the time, I find the argument circular and (from personal experience) implausible. The second element is gaining general acceptance. Even so, White does appreciate volition being transcended either in an emotional state (such as fear or excitement) and in a 'low dynamic intensity state'. This latter state is achieved, as we have pointed out, by activating the parasympathetic nervous system. What is clear is that it is important to suspend reality testing and reduce the sensory input in order to activate the parasympathetic nervous system (although not put this way either by White or Shor).

In Sarbin's extension[40] of White's theory he emphasizes role-playing. In other words, the special orientation required for hypnosis is one where the self is submerged and the person behaves *as-if*. This is a fairly common treatment of hypnosis.

By submerging the self the reality-orientation is relinquished. When this is done no testing against preconceived notions of reality is undertaken. If this is successful then the only reality is that being presented to the senses.

As we point out in Chapter 2, when discussing recent research on the brain, there is a blocking action of the orienting reflex when an environment becomes familiar. The induction procedures of hypnosis do just this. When induction is successful it is the *conditioned reflex* which becomes activated. This activation can come about through verbal suggestion. These changes are not brought about in the cortex but rather in the relationship between the cortex and the reticular activating system (RAS). The slow, repetitive and melodious induction seems to bring this change about. Once the conditioned reflex is established the reality-orientation is bypassed and role-playing can take place. In autohypnosis this is accomplished by the same individual. What makes autohypnosis more difficult than heterohypnosis is that the self-suggestions prolong the reality-orienting state of mind. Alternatively, the self-suggestions raise difficulties in submerging the self. However, if the suggestions are kept up, eventually the conditioned reflex comes into action. With repeated use the conditioned reflex is easier to activate and so the autohypnotist will find it easier to submerge the self. The main reason why some individuals find it difficult to enter hypnosis is because of their reluctance to 'let go of reality'. It seems that this satisfies some psychological need. More to the point, the training one has over a lifetime is in creating a reality-orientation. In hypnosis the reverse process is required. Some people are more flexible and adept at changing their orientation than others. (Just as some people can drive backwards better than others!) The more adaptable a person is, the easier the self can be submerged and the easier the hypnotic state can be achieved.

A number of the points just made come out in the experiences of Huxley, referred to above. Huxley always went into a state of *deep reflection* in the same chair, so creating the right mental state. He could prolong the state when he had something specific to think about but would come out of it when he had nothing to think about. Just as conscious awareness requires constant stimuli, so does the hypnotic state. If no suggestions are made then this will either lead to natural sleep or to awakening consciousness. Furthermore, attempts to explore the subjective state of hypnosis is likely to deepen it still further. This is probably because it sets up a closed loop. It could also be that as the reticular activating system affects the cortex to induce the hypnosis, the cortex influences the RAS by thoughts and so reinforces the state, hence the individual goes deeper into hypnosis. Huxley himself found he had a subjective need to go deeper into hypnosis but an intellectual need to stay in a light trance. As Baudouin points out, the stronger emotion will win out. Finally, the reality-orientation was experienced when Huxley was asked to examine a chair objectively. When he did this his hypnotic state became lighter. If, on the other hand, he was asked to examine the chair subjectively (e.g., its softness) then the state became deeper. The explanation of this is likely to be that the left brain is more involved in objective evaluation while the right brain is more involved in subjective evaluation. The depth of hypnosis seems to be connected with the need or not on some people's part to have some link with objective reality – in simple terms, with how difficult they find it to 'let go' of reality.

What we observe from the foregoing discussion is the importance of the self in reality-orientation and the sub-mergence of the self in ASCs. We may go further and argue that there are many selves, each one appropriate to a particular state of consciousness. Let us for a moment suppose there are many selves, but you consider there is only the one – the real self. It is clear, then, that you are in a sense imprisoned in that self. There is no existence other than this reality and only the self in that reality. Plato's cave immediately comes to mind here. A set of prisoners have lived all their lives in a cave with their backs to the entrance and the shadows of people passing are thrown onto the wall in front. Their only reality is the shadows on the wall. One day one of them escapes and sees that the shadows are merely reflections of the people outside. It is the people outside which is the true reality. When he informs his friends in the cave they take him to be insane! The same idea is pursued in H. G. Wells' short story of the man who could see in the village of the blind.

By accepting the *possibility* of many selves it becomes easier to submerge the self of reality-orientation. One reason for this is that if you believe in only one true self then there is a subconscious need not to eliminate this self – to do so, in a sense, is to die. If, however, the submergence of the reality self allows the emergence of another self, then the subconscious fear no longer exists so strongly. (It may still exist in some form because of the uncertainty attached to the other selves.) Now this is *not* the same as multiple personality, which is a psychological abnormality. The multiple personality is a *fragmented* self and not another self; it is a fragmenting of the self which creates the reality-orientation. Because the mind may become so fragmented, only some of the personalities are consciously aware of particular aspects of reality.

Once the possibility of many selves is accepted then a totally new way of thinking and behaving opens up to the individual. Consider, for instance, the following quotation from Ropp[37.] on dealing with anxiety.

> The student of Creative Psychology does not attempt to eliminate anxiety of this kind. He simply observes, striving as far as possible, to separate his sense of 'I' from the physical sensations he is studying. After a while, he makes a very curious discovery. The effort to observe and, at the same time, not to identify with the sensations he is studying little by little changes those sensations. Without directly trying to do so (how can one 'try' not to feel anxiety?), he has learned how to control the reaction. For the fact is (as the student can confirm for himself) that observation, which means bringing a sensation into the focus of awareness, alters the process itself. It brings about a definite change in the nervous pathways that are operating to produce the anxiety. It switches the energy into a different channel. So one who sets out with a firm intention: 'I am going to observe carefully the physical sensations of this thing I call anxiety,' discovers to his surprise that there is no anxiety left to observe. (p.151).

All this would make no sense if one did not accept the possibility of many selves.

The main difficulty about the concept of self, from the point of view of autohypnosis, is that there are many such theories. They do, however, have one thing in common – they accept that there is more than one self. Given this, then the autohypnotist should have less worry in his attempts to submerge the conscious self, for only by so doing will his hypnotic state be successful.

Summary
Let us see where we have arrived at for the autohypnotist. We

shall do this in the form of a list:

(1) Autohypnosis is an ASC which is self-induced.

(2) Autohypnosis involves the construction of a special temporary orientation on a small range of topics and a suspension or reduction of the generalized-reality orientation.

(3) Positive autohypnosis involves activating the parasympathetic nervous system.

(4) Autohypnosis is a subjective state.

(5) The switch away from generalized-reality orientation means a switch from the left to the right hemisphere of the brain.

(6) Hypnotic tests of depth (discussed in Chapter 5) not only test but actually deepen the hypnotic state. They do this because they reinforce the special temporary orientation by activating the right brain.

(7) Any activity while in the hypnotic state which utilizes right brain features (e.g., imagery, emotion, etc.) will reinforce the hypnotic state.

(8) Hypnosis requires the suppression of the self in order to relinquish the reality-orientation and attain an appropriate ASC.

4.
Personality Correlates

Can everyone be hypnotized? Is there a type of person who is more hypnotizable than another person? Both of these questions have been repeatedly asked and answers sought to them without any real success. The question, 'Can everyone be hypnotized?' is a question about absolutes. Either everyone can be hypnotized or only some people can be hypnotized. Whatever the answer to this question, there still remains the second question, 'Is there a type of person who is more hypnotizable than another person?' This is a matter of degree. There is, however, some overlap between the two questions.

If everyone can be hypnotized then there is the problem of explaining why some induction procedures do not succeed. If only some people can be hypnotized then an explanation must be sought to determine why, and whether we can predict which category any given individual will belong to: whether to the hypnotizable or to the non-hypnotizable. Whether we are attempting to explain why some induction procedures do not work with some individuals or whether we are attempting to explain why some people are not hypnotizable, we are grouping people into personality categories. Put another way, we wish to know what personality characteristics are associated (correlated) with hypnotizability.

There is one major difficulty with such an association. Not only do we not know exactly what hypnosis is, but there is no agreed classification of personality. Of course, the simplest way to know whether someone is hypnotizable is actually to hypnotize them. The attempt to find correlates with hypnosis is in order to predict who will be hypnotizable. What is not so readily appreciated is that it also gives some insight as to why a particular person does not respond to a specific induction technique or to a particular hypnotist. Furthermore, it gives the autohypnotist some insight into the difficulties he may encounter in attempting self-hypnosis. For the autohypnotist there is only his own personality to contend with. But because it *is* his own personality, this is more difficult to assess in an objective manner. Even so, some of the more obvious personality correlates with hypnosis do not require a deep understanding of personality since they are largely to do with involvement: involvement in art, music, reading, etc.

Is Everyone Hypnotizable?

This is not at all an easy question to answer. Part of the reason for this is because we do not know exactly what hypnosis is. Suppose I said to you there is a disease, the exact symptoms of which we do not know, and I then ask whether everyone can fall victim to such a disease. This would be almost impossible to answer – in just the same way that it is impossible to answer whether everyone is hypnotizable. When a person is not hypnotized by someone then we must establish whether:

1. It is because the person cannot be hypnotized
2. The induction technique is inappropriate
3. The subject objects to the hypnotist (consciously or unconsciously)

First let us discuss the second and third reasons.

There are a number of induction techniques for inducing hypnosis, either in oneself or in another person, a number of which are discussed in Hartland,[18] Kroger[24] and Shone.[41] But why not just have one technique? The reason is that some people respond to one technique and not to another. The major personality correlate in this respect is whether the induction technique is authoritarian or not and whether the person being hypnotized does or does not like such an attitude. Suppose, for instance, the hypnotist is using an authoritarian approach and the person being hypnotized objects to this – either consciously or unconsciously. For example, the hypnotist may say 'you are getting drowsy', 'you will now go to sleep', 'you will not be able to open your eyes', and so on. These are authoritarian statements which also involve a challenge. If in your early childhood you had constantly been told to do this, and to do that, then you are likely to resent in later life being told to do things. Some may resent it so much that they are inclined to do the very opposite. If this was so then that person may not enter hypnosis. This is not because they are not hypnotizable, but rather because they resent the technique being used. If the suggestions were changed to something like the following then they would be far less authoritarian. 'Let yourself go, I would like you to feel very relaxed and drowsy. You will find that if you let yourself relax that you will soon feel yourself going into a deep sleep. Your eyes are so heavy that you will not want to open them, and that when you try to open them the heaviness is going to increase. You may find that your eyes open, but what is important is that they feel heavy and that you don't feel like opening them.' Yet in other people, the authoritarian attitude is the very approach which works.

In general the actual technique is not so important. Most people respond to any technique. The problem arises when a person does not respond to a particular induction technique. It is then that different techniques must be tried. Some people respond very well to the beat of a metronome while others find it positively annoying; some respond very well to music, but only if it is of the right type; and yet others respond well to induction techniques where they are physically involved, rather than depending on mere suggestions while concentrating on a fixed point.

To some extent the success of a particular induction technique may depend on the person's expectation. If a person expects the hypnotist to swing some shiny object in front of them, then this is the technique which is likely to have the most success *with that person*. In other cases the appropriate technique is found by trial and improvisation. The fact that improvisation often works reveals that it is not the actual technique which is important – except in inducing hypnosis in a given individual. Whether hypnosis is induced by someone else, or by yourself, improvised techniques only need to be resorted to if the standard induction procedures fail to work.

In the case of heterohypnosis the induction may fail to work, not because the technique is inappropriate, but rather because the person being hypnotized takes exception to the hypnotist. This may be conscious or unconscious. For instance, a person may not like to be hypnotized by a hypnotist of the opposite sex; by a hypnotist that smokes (when they are a nonsmoker); by a hypnotist that looks like their mother (or father); by a hypnotist with a beard; and so on. The list can be quite long. While the person is willing to be hypnotized and the technique is not objectionable, this will not generally be the case. But when a person does not enter hypnosis this is always a possibility. *For the autohypnotist this is not the situation.*

However, suppose the technique is appropriate and the hypnotist is not objectionable, is it still possible for a person not to enter hypnosis? In other words, is it possible for a person not to be hypnotizable by anyone or any technique?

It is common to read and hear that about seventy per cent of the population is hypnotizable. I would consider this figure a gross underestimate. In the first instance it is based on samples using a fixed technique and a particular hypnotist. Second, the figure is often based on only one attempt. Given the different personalities of the persons being hypnotized, some will not readily enter hypnosis until a number of their fears and (misguided) preconceived notions are allayed.

Part of the difficulty is the belief that you either can be or cannot be hypnotized: that you are A or not-A. But this makes sense only if hypnosis were a well-defined entity, which we have already indicated that it is not, (only when A is well defined do we know what not-A means). Let us agree for the moment that hypnosis is an altered state of consciousness (or a number of altered states), as we have argued previously. Then we can re-phase the question, 'Can everyone be hypnotized?' as, 'Can everyone alter appropriately their state of consciousness?' When put in this way it is clear that entering hypnosis (hypnotic susceptibility) is a learning process, that it is the acquisition of an ability. *A person learns to enter hypnosis.* When looked at in this way, then it is a matter of degree and not an absolute. Some people will find the learning process easy and others will find it difficult. There is a whole spectrum of abilities in learning to enter (and deepen) hypnosis. I would liken it to asking the question, 'Can everyone play tennis?' The answer is, in general, yes but some can play better than others.

There are of course some exceptions. Because hypnosis depends very much on verbal suggestion, very young children (about up to the age of four) cannot be hypnotized. In addition anyone, for whatever reason, who cannot maintain concentration will also be very difficult or impossible to hypnotize. This is because if the suggestions are to take root in the unconscious mind then the person must be capable of holding the suggestion in their mind for a sufficient length of time. Thus, imbeciles and some people with mental disorders cannot be hypnotized. It is worth explaining the reason why in more detail, because this will also explain why some people find entering hypnosis difficult.

In Chapter 2 we mentioned that the cortex of the brain is divided into two hemispheres separated by the corpus callosum. The hypnotic induction is a means of reducing the functioning of the left hemisphere of the brain and activating the right hemisphere. The point is that language is largely a left brain attribute and what is required in hypnosis is that the suggestions pass very quickly into the right hemisphere of the brain *without activating the cortex of the left hemisphere*. The conjecture being advanced here is that this is accomplished by first concentrating on the suggestions until an habituation reflex is established. Once this is established the suggestions will be paid no particular attention by the conscious mind, but will still be processed by the unconscious mind. For this process to occur it requires that the person is capable of concentrating on the suggestions and yet paying them no particular attention. In other words, habituation is a learning process. To the extent that some people find it difficult to 'let go' we can interpret this to mean that they do not wish to lose conscious control, that they do not wish to allow habituation to take place. This conjecture is supported, to some extent, by the work of Dr Gruzelier, which we outline on page 35.

Habituation is a feature of the nervous system that is possessed by everyone. There is no such thing as possessing no habituation. There may, however, be difficulty in bringing such habituation under conscious control: the ability to choose to habituate or not. Imbeciles and young children cannot habituate out of choice. Other people will have varying degrees of difficulty in doing so. Of course, we should not fall into the trap of assuming that hypnosis and habituation are the same thing. The ability to habituate means only that a person is susceptible to hypnosis: that the person can enter hypnosis. It does not guarantee that the person will, in fact, enter hypnosis. The only point being advanced here is that because almost everyone can habituate then almost everyone can be hypnotized. Whether they actually enter hypnosis is quite a different matter.

If the argument being advanced here is accepted then it follows that the depth of hypnosis is also connected with the ability to habituate. We shall take up the issue of hypnotic depth in the next chapter.

Introversion, Extroversion and Hypnotizability

One of the main categorizations of personality is that put forward by Jung. He divided people into two main groups: the introverts and the extroverts. Introverts tend to draw into themselves, tend to be on their own and are often shy. They are dominated by feelings, emotions and situations from within. Extroverts tend to seek the company of others and are usually very sociable, they tend to choose jobs and situations which involve other people. Extroverts are dominated by feelings, emotions and situations from without. Of course, these are the two ends of the spectrum. A given individual will probably have a mixture of the two and lie somewhere between these two extremes.

From our present point of view the question of interest is, 'Is the extrovert more readily hypnotizable than the introvert?' One way to assess this is to find a scale for measuring both extroversion/introversion and hypnotizability and then establishing the statistical correlation between the two groups. But neither extroversion/introversion nor hypnotizability are clear enough categories from which to establish agreed measures. In this case it is not possible to carry out such a measure with any success. (It is always possible to carry out some statistical exercise, but the question remains whether the results are at all meaningful!) Furthermore, much of the information that has been obtained on hypnotizability has been carried out in the psychology departments of universities. The samples are therefore undergraduate students, and these are not necessarily representative of the public at large.

Even so, there is a general belief that extroverts probably are more hypnotizable than introverts. There is no scientific basis for this belief. One of the real problems with hypnosis is whether we are confusing hypnosis with compliance. Wagstaff[47] has argued that much of hypnosis is compliance. To the extent that an extrovert likes to please when in the company of others, then he is more likely to agree to 'play along', to be compliant. But this raises the question of what the difference is between compliance, susceptibility and hypnosis.

We pointed out in the previous section that the ability to enter hypnosis (and probably the depth of hypnosis) is, in all likelihood, connected with a person's ability to habituate. One reason why there may be no clear correlation between extroversion/introversion and hypnotizability is because there is no inherent reason why an extrovert should be more capable of habituating than an introvert. The reason and motivation to habituate may be different for the two categories, but what matters for hypnosis is that they can, in fact, habituate. This is an important conclusion for the self-hypnotist. Whether you are extrovert or introvert does not really make any difference to your ability to enter hypnosis.

Before leaving this particular topic it may be worth mentioning

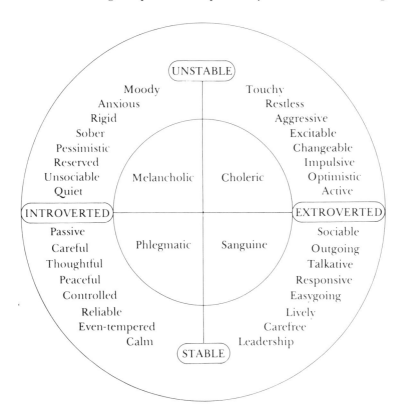

Figure 4

Source: H. J. Eysenck, *You and Neurosis*

the work of Hans Eysenck. He classifies personality not just by extroversion/introversion but also by stability/instability. This latter division is concerned with a person's emotional state, varying at one end from calm, well-adjusted and reliable to moody, anxious, and unreliable. The various traits associated with this double classification are shown in Figure 4. Most individuals would be somewhere in the centre of the circle. But even this is a static interpretation of an individual. Let us suppose an individual is represented by a point. There is no reason why such a point should remain in the same position. As a person changes and responds to life's changes so he may move from one position to another. One of the purposes of self-improvement is, in fact, to move yourself around the circle to a position you consider better. This dynamic interpretation can also explain why the same individual responds and feels different when entering hypnosis on different occasions.

Hypnotizability and Involvement

One avenue of investigation is that of Josephine Hilgard who has attempted to investigate the correlation between involvement and hypnotizability.[20, 21] This line of research is especially useful for the self-hypnotist because it will also give some insight into how to *improve* hypnotic susceptibility.

She considers a number of paths into hypnosis: reading, dramatic arts, aesthetic involvement, religious dedication and adventure. A person may have one or more of these paths into hypnosis. She contends, however, that susceptibility to hypnosis is *no* greater when there is more than one path than if there were only one.

It is not my intention here to discuss her statistical work in detail. What I wish to do is indicate something about the type of involvement and attempt to explain why there is likely to be a correlation between involvement and hypnotizability. It must be emphasized again that these are purely conjectures since our knowledge, both of hypnosis and personality, is not sufficiently developed at the present time to substantiate them.

Rather than consider each involvement in turn we shall simply consider them together and emphasize the difference between them. People involve themselves in reading in different ways. Some people identify themselves with the hero or heroine in the novel (or even a biography). They can do this on two levels. One is where they can take on the same feelings and emotions as the hero or heroine because they are that person. Others consider the hero or heroine as if from the point of view of a third person. They do not identify exactly with them but are emotionally influenced, as they would be if the situation occurred in real life and they were looking on as an observer. These two forms of identification also arise in the dramatic arts. An actor, in particular, can take on the emotions and feelings of the person he or she is portraying. They identify themselves with that person. This partially explains why children are such good hypnotic subjects. Many children like play acting, and some even have imaginary playmates.

The important point about this type of involvement is that such individuals suppress their 'self' and take on the characteristics of the other person: they allow themselves to become someone else temporarily. They of course know that they are not the person in the book, but the book is much more enjoyable if they experience what the hero or heroine is experiencing. Similarly, the actor knows that he/she is not the person he/she is portraying, but the part can only be 'realistic' if he/she suppresses as far as possible his/her own self and take on the other character. This is not just a feature of actors. We all do it to some extent when we present to other people different parts of our own character. The man at work may be different from the man at home, and both may be different from the man who socializes. This is the basis of Berne's *Games People Play*[4] and of transactional analysis.

Another feature of great importance is the ability to fantasize. This is not only a suppression of the self, but it also involves a suspension of reality. This is most obvious to people who enjoy reading science fiction novels or fantasy novels. In reading these they may not identify with any of the characters, but rather simply become absorbed in the fantasy. Such absorption, such involvement, can occur to varying degrees, depending on how well the reader can suspend reality and enter the world that the author is creating. One important aspect of this suspension of reality is that the pleasure or pain is immediate to the reader. The reader may be reading about the past, the present, or even some unknown place at an unknown time, but they are experiencing the feelings created by the writer *immediately*. This is worth commenting on further.

Reality-testing is a feature of the left hemisphere of the brain. One of the points about reality-testing is that the brain compares any incoming information with what it has already encountered in the past with regard to the environment. If I begin reading about a hobbit then there is no reality to compare this against because it is unreal. I can process the information in a logical fashion by comparing it with previous occasions where I have read about a hobbit. But this is a process of analysis and not what I want when I read a novel. The right hemisphere of the brain, however, does not require any reality to carry out its functions. It merely responds to images that are created in the mind. More to the point, the responses are immediate: you are sad now, happy now, and joyful now. You cannot delay an emotion. You can delay a decision, which is a feature of the left hemisphere of the brain, but you cannot delay an emotion, which is a feature of the right hemisphere of the brain. Part of the reason for this is that when you have an emotion your body must be activated in a way which is consistent with the emotion. Breathing may alter, hormonal activity may alter and blood-pressure may change. These changes can be activated by an image in the right hemisphere of the brain. The right hemisphere does not question whether the image is real or whether the environment that is being suggested to it actually exists. It simply responds. This is why a number of writers have considered that the subconscious mind operates like a psycho-cybernetic.[28, 39] A faulty image, or different image of ourselves, will create body responses and conscious responses consistent with such an image. So when a person is reading a science fiction novel or a fantasy story they can become emotionally involved in it if they can suppress the reality-testing of the left hemisphere of the brain. By so doing they enjoy the story much more.

Religious commitment appears to engender quite a different aspect that can facilitate hypnosis. A person who is religiously committed practises belief and also allows himself to be subject to authority. To some extent this is also true of people in the armed forces and students. Hilgard[21] puts it as follows:

> Here we have the interplay of identification, of joyful participation, of basic trust, of respect for benevolent authority. With these attitudes engendered in early childhood and continued with institutional and parental support, it is easy to accept the demands

of hypnosis, the confidence in trusted authority, the lack of questioning when unfamiliar elements are introduced into prosaic reality. (p.74)

Hilgard considers also the adventurer as a path to hypnosis. These are individuals who are willing to tolerate danger and disapproval in order to explore the unknown, who have a curiosity about the ranges of human experiences. These experiences may be physical in nature – such as skiing, skin-diving, and mountain climbing (basically non-competitive sports in which the experience gives rise to immediate emotion); or they may be mental – such as taking drugs, having their fortunes told, or experimenting in expanded mind consciousness. They all have in common the desire for a new and different experience beyond the ordinary, whether physical or mental. What does appear to be the case is a rise in the number of people engaging in 'mental games', and what M. Ferguson has labelled *The Aquarian Conspiracy*.[14]

It should be noted that all these paths to hypnosis activate, in one way or another, the right hemisphere of the brain. What appears on the surface to be a different collection of human experiences, on more detailed observation turns out to be simply different attributes and functions of the right hemisphere of the brain. Once again, this does not mean that if a person does lose themselves in reading a novel, or is an actor, or is devoutly religious, or is adventurous that they will automatically enter hypnosis. It only means that they should, other things being equal, enter hypnosis with more ease than a person who does not do any of these things.

What can the autohypnotist learn from these investigations?

(1) Learn to identify with a person in any novel that you are reading. Learn to experience the emotion that the writer is giving the hero or heroine; with practice this can improve. It is not a question of whether you can or you can't. Everyone can, but to different degrees. Like many things, it is a learning process (or even of doing once again what you did in your youth).

(2) Improve your fantasizing, whether in the form of science fiction or in the form of fantasy stories. Although some people do not like science fiction, they occasionally like fantasy stories. If you dislike both, and you find it difficult to enter self-hypnosis, then this may be the reason. Your hold on reality is so great that you refuse to engage in such 'silly' pursuits.

(3) Belief is a most powerful force. If you believe that you can hypnotize yourself then this will be a major element in succeeding. You must eliminate any doubts and negative thoughts about the procedure and have confidence in both yourself and in your ability to achieve hypnosis. This does not necessarily mean that you will be successful immediately. It means only that it will work given time, patience and knowledge.

(4) Learn to be adventurous – either physically, mentally or both. In terms of mental adventures this does not necessarily mean taking drugs. There are a number of ways to achieve expanded mind consciousness without the use of drugs, typical examples of which are Masters and Houston's *Mind Games*[30] and the author's *Creative Visualization*.[42]

Conclusion

The conclusion to draw from the above discussion is that there is no obvious personality type which is more hypnotizable than other types. If you believe that introverts cannot be hypnotized, and you are an introvert, then this will create an expectation of lack of success. It is not the fact of being introverted that prevents you from being hypnotized but rather your erroneous belief. Television, films and books give rise to many erroneous beliefs about hypnosis which can prevent you from achieving such a state. You must enter the process with an open mind and an expectation of success. Nothing in the literature has established any clear correlation which is indisputable. The paths to hypnosis discussed by Hilgard, although interesting and revealing, are also not without criticism. But they do indicate the importance of activating the right hemisphere of the brain, which is a point we stress throughout this book. That such tests are often not statistically significant (i.e., in terms of standard statistical testing procedures) is not necessarily an indication that there is no correlation, but rather that the attributes being examined are not readily quantifiable. How do you measure 'adventurous'? If you cannot measure either adventurous or hypnotizability then how can you possibly measure any correlation between the two! This is not meant as a criticism against such studies, it is meant as a caution, given our present state of knowledge.

5.
Measuring Hypnotic Depth

In this chapter the intention is to consider a number of studies which have been undertaken on measuring the depth of hypnotic trance. On the face of it, this may appear a discussion which is out of place in a book on self-hypnosis. But the self-hypnotist is often concerned about how deep he should go and often wants to know how deep he actually is. Our intention is not to get involved in a critical analysis of the tests themselves, but to use the various tests as a means of discussing the relevance or otherwise of hypnotic depth. In other words: does it matter how deep you go? If the answer is 'Yes', then the next question is: how do I know when I am deep enough? It is the tests into hypnotic depth which help us to answer these questions.

Does Hypnotic Depth Matter?
Before discussing the tests for hypnotic depth, the individual who has engaged in hypnosis will know *from personal experience* that the depth will vary from session to session without any deliberate suggestion about hypnotic depth. This should not be at all surprising. The brain and the body are dynamic: they change from moment to moment. This is true even when a person is not hypnotized at all. Some days you feel good, while other days you do not. Some days you can make decisions easily while other days you cannot. Your physiology and your consciousness change from moment to moment. Just as your moods change during normal consciousness, so they also change during hypnotic sessions. This means that no two hypnotic sessions are alike. Some hypnotic sessions will be deeper than others for no obvious reason.

But does it matter how deep you go during a hypnotic

session? This is not an easy question to answer because the answer partly depends on what you wish to do during the hypnosis. For instance, if you simply wanted to lose weight and you were giving yourself suggestions to do this, then it is not necessary for you to go very deeply into hypnosis. The tests indicate that success is achieved even in light and medium hypnosis. The self-hypnotist will know from personal experience that their suggestions lead to changing behaviour, even when they are in a light to medium trance. What matters is the success in the objective and not in the depth of the trance. If you wish to achieve objective X and you can do this in light, medium or deep hypnosis, then what matters is that you achieve X and not the greatest depth of hypnosis before trying to achieve X. It is, in fact, possible to achieve objective X sometimes only in deep hypnosis, while at other times it can be achieved in medium hypnosis. The reason is that the depth of hypnosis is only *one* requirement for the success of a particular suggestion or therapy. Motivation and general health may be other reasons for success or failure. To argue that you must be at a particular depth is to suppose that the success of a suggestion or therapy is associated *only* with hypnotic depth. All the evidence indicates that this is not the case. Wolberg[51] puts it as follows, 'Generally, we may say that there is no correlation between the depth of trance and the effectiveness of therapeutic suggestions.' (p.74) There is nothing intrinsically interesting about a particular depth (except to the scientific investigator). What is of interest is achieving some stated aim.

The test procedures, to be discussed below, indicate depth according to which tests are passed. You could then be classified according to such a test as having been in light, medium or deep hypnosis. But this is purely of interest to the scientist. I am not arguing against such testing, what is important for the self-hypnotist is the evidence that there does not appear to be any correlation between the achievement of some objective and the depth of trance. If such a test is undertaken and you were recorded as being in, say, a medium trance, this does not mean that you *cannot* go into a deep trance. All that has been established is that on this particular day, and during this particular test, you entered only a medium trance. This does not classify you for ever! Even so, it does not help you in any way in knowing how deep you should go in order, say, to suggest to yourself that you are going to succeed in learning a foreign language, to perform well at an interview, to relax during a minor surgical operation, to improve your typing skills, and so on.

As we shall see, the tests do give us some guide in establishing what depth is necessary for certain aims. But if you had no such information, there is one thing you can do. *You can learn to go as deep as possible over a period of time.* Doing this will aid in those suggestions where a deeper depth is necessary. But no aim is automatically to be associated with a particular depth and only that depth. Other factors, along with depth, will determine whether the suggestions will be successful. To repeat, there is nothing inherent in the depth itself, what matters is being able to achieve some stated objective.

There are two ways of looking at the depth of hypnosis. First, by making observations of the hypnotized person. Second, by undertaking recognized tests of the hypnotized person. We shall take each of these in turn.

Clinical Observations of Depth

In the case of heterohypnosis, the hypnotist can obtain some idea of the depth of trance of the hypnotized person by considering some recognized, changing patterns of behaviour.

When a person is entering hypnosis a common (but not universal) observation is that the person's eyelids flicker. As they go deeper this flickering stops. At the same time, the person's eyes roll upwards. Of course, these observations will only be noticed if the induction procedure begins with the eyes open and the subject is attempting to achieve eye closure – which is by far the most common induction procedure. If the induction begins with the eyes closed, the hypnotist may still observe flickering of the eyelids which stops as the hynosis deepens.

A second observation is that the head rolls to one side or forwards as the hypnosis deepens. This is because the head is very heavy and as the person begins to relax the head cannot be supported in an upright position. This can lead to strain in some of the neck muscles which will prevent the hypnosis from going deeper still; but for many people this is not a problem. Other characteristics of the increased relaxation are drooping shoulders, a more expressionless face (as the facial muscles relax) and possibly the mouth opening as the jaw relaxes. This is also accompanied by slow and low speech – if speech is requested by the hypnotist. In addition, breathing becomes slow, deep and steady. In fact, all these are typical of a person relaxing. The point is that, as the hypnosis deepens, the person begins to close off the left hemisphere of the brain and as this occurs the person begins to 'let go'. This 'letting go' means that the person is not letting the mind control the body at the conscious level. As the person relaxes there is less need for the mind to concern itself with the body. It does not have to make (conscious) decisions about which arm to lift up, where to go, what to eat, etc. Because the conscious (left) brain has nothing to concern itself with – except the instructions of the hypnotist – it can shut itself down to a large extent. This shutting down produces the increased depth and the characteristic body changes that we have just mentioned.

Now all of these changes are what the hypnotist observes in the person being hypnotized. In the case of autohypnosis the person cannot make such *visual* observations. Of course, the autohypnotist can make experiential observations. He will be aware of his eyelids flickering and then the flickering stopping. He will be aware of his head rolling to one side. He will be aware of the relaxation in his facial muscles. He will be aware of his shoulders drooping and his muscles becoming heavy (or in some people light). He will be aware that his breathing is becoming deeper and steadier. All these are characteristic of the hypnotic trance deepening. It is important, however, that the autohypnotist does not pay any attention to these experiences.

But the person being hypnotized can also experience other sensations which are not visible to the hypnotist. One of the most conspicuous is a feeling of heaviness in the limbs (although some people feel the opposite, namely a lightness in the limbs). This may be accompanied by a tingling sensation also in the limbs, although this tingling sensation passes. Even though the eyes are closed and it appears 'dark', this darkness gets more intense as the hypnosis deepens. In addition, a feeling of detachment occurs, which also increases in intensity as the hypnosis deepens. It is possible to reach a point where you feel as though you are just 'pure thought'. In other words, you have no conscious awareness of your body and you are simply thought.

But as we pointed out above, one should not assume that only when you achieve detachment are you deeply hypnotized.

The fallacy in this can be appreciated by realizing that in hypnosis you could suggest to yourself that you are acutely aware of your physical existence; that is to say, that you are acutely aware of your muscles, your legs and arms, your chest, your breathing and all those features you associate with your physical existence. This is most revealing when it is undertaken because it gives you a different and much more intense awareness of your physical existence than you would get at the conscious level. The reason is not simply that you are focusing your mind on your physical existence, which of course you are doing, but because you are in a relaxed state and so all your energy is being directed to your awareness of your physical body. Both right and left hemispheres of the brain are being brought into operation in this activity – and more importantly, they are co-operating with one another.

Ultimately, the only way to decide whether you are going deeper is to consider whether there is any qualitative change taking place over a *number* of hypnotic sessions. This is not an unreasonable statement. Going into a hypnotic state, whether in heterohypnosis or autohypnosis, is a learning process. *You learn to enter and deepen hypnosis.* Now if you had had three sessions of tennis and I asked you whether your game had improved, you probably would say 'possibly'. In the first instance, three games are too few to make such a judgement at all accurately; and second, you would have difficulty in explaining how you know that your game has or has not improved.

Hypnotizability Scales

A widely-used scale for testing the depth of hypnosis is the Barber suggestibility scale. In the first instance it should be noted that strictly this refers to the degree of suggestibility. At the same time, however, a number of the suggestions could not (in general) take place in the waking state – although Barber has usually claimed that all actions done in hypnosis can be performed in the normal waking state.

In Table 4 we supply the eight test suggestions given in the Barber scale.[2] Responses to the test suggestions are scored in two ways: *objectively* and *subjectively*. In the objective scoring, if subjects pass the test then they are given a score of 1 for that particular test and 0 if they do not pass it. The criterion for passing each test is given in the final column of Table 4.

Hence, on the Barber suggestibility scale the total score ranges from 0 (none of the tests were passed) to 8 (all tests were passed).

Table 4

Test Suggestion	Description of Test	Criterion for Passing Test
1 Arm lowering	Beginning with arms extended and horizontal, suggest for 30 secs that arm is becoming heavy and is moving down.	Arm moved down 4 or more inches.
2 Arm levitation	Beginning with left arm horizontal suggest for 30 secs that arm is weightless and is moving up.	Arm moved up 4 or more inches.
3 Hand lock	After clasping hands with fingers intertwined, suggest for 45 secs that hands are welded together and cannot be taken apart.	He failed to unclasp his hands after 15 secs of trying to do so.
4 Thirst hallucination	Subject told repeatedly for 45 secs that he is becoming extremely thirsty.	He showed observable signs of thirst, such as moistening his lips, marked mouth movements, or swallowing, and stated that he felt thirsty.
5 Verbal inhibition	Suggest for 45 secs that the subject's throat and jaw muscles are rigid and he cannot speak his name.	He did not say his name even though he tried to say it for at least 15 secs.
6 Body immobility	Suggest for 45 secs that the subject's body is heavy and rigid and he cannot stand up.	He was not standing erect from the chair after 15 secs of trying to stand erect.
7 Posthypnotic-like response	Subject told that, when the experiment is over, he will cough automatically when he hears a click.	He coughed or cleared his throat post-experimentally when presented with the click stimulus.

8 Selective amnesia	Subject told that when experiment is over, he will remember all of the test suggestions except the one instructing him to move his arm up (arm levitation), and then he will remember this test suggestion when he is given a cue word.	He did not refer to the item which was to be forgotten, but mentioned at least 4 other items and then recalled the 'forgotten' item when given the cue word.

Subjects' responses are also scored subjectively. After each test the subject is asked whether they actually experienced each suggested effect or simply went along with the suggestion in order to comply with the instructions, or to please the experimenter. If the subject claims that he actually experienced the suggested effect then he is given a score of 1, otherwise he is given a score of 0 for that particular test. Again the scale ranges from 0 (none of the tests were experienced) to 8 (all of the tests were experienced).

It should be noted that many of the tests are used quite frequently during induction procedures to gauge the depth to which a person is hypnotized. It is usually presumed that tests further down the list require greater depth in order to accomplish them. Something that experimenters often do not take account of is that the very act of doing some of the tests will itself deepen the hypnosis. In other words, the depth is not fixed during the experiment. However, this may not be too serious because the duration of any suggestion is relatively small, as indicated by the second column in Table 4. On the other hand, what may matter in considering the depth of hypnosis is not the duration of each *individual* test, but rather the duration of the *whole* test.

One popular division of hypnosis is into light, medium and deep hypnosis. There is one test procedure[8] where hypnosis is classified into five main states. The only reason for reporting this here is that it reveals what is usually classified under the umbrella of light, medium and deep hypnosis. The five main states are given in Table 5. The authors point out that their quantitative index is arbitrary. But what they further point out is their belief that subjects pass gradually through the list: that there are no large steps but simply gradual increments.

Implicit, rather than explicit, is that in general subjects go through the list in the order in which the authors have presented them.

Table 5

Hypnotic Susceptibility Scoring System

Depth	Score	Objective Symptoms
Insusceptible	0	
Hypnoidal	1	
	2	Relaxation
	3	Fluttering of lids
	4	Closing of eyes
	5	Complete physical relaxation
Light Trance	6	Catalepsy of eyes
	7	Limb catalepsies
	10	Rigid catalepsy
	11	Anaesthesia (glove)
Medium Trance	13	Partial amnesia
	15	Post-hypnotic anaesthesia
	17	Personality changes
	18	Simple post-hypnotic suggestions
	20	Kinaesthetic delusions; complete amnesia
Somnambulistic Trance	21	Ability to open eyes without affecting trance
	23	Bizarre post-hypnotic suggestions
	25	Complete somnambulism
	26	Positive visual hallucinations, post-hypnotic
	27	Positive auditory hallucinations, post-hypnotic
	28	Systematized post-hypnotic amnesia
	29	Negative auditory hallucinations
	30	Negative visual hallucinations; hyper-aesthesias

Source: Davis and Husband (1958)

The Barber suggestibility scale does indicate the two most popular methods of scoring: namely, objective tests and those often referred to as 'self-report scales'. The self-report scales, and there are quite a number (especially in the United States), do require that the person knows what hypnosis is and knows how to report his experiences. For this reason they have been strongly criticized. But even the objective tests are set up in terms of some view about what hypnosis is and, as we have already pointed out, there is no single view as to what hypnosis actually is.

Even from these brief comments, the conclusion that can be

drawn is that there is no simple way to measure the depth of hypnosis. There is no guarantee that during the experiment itself the depth will remain constant – and if it does not, then what is it that is being measured! Subjects themselves are not sure what to expect and their expectations will almost certainly influence any subjective report on a particular test.

The main point about any test is the usual scientific requirement that the test be objective – and by that it is meant that it should be independent of the experimenter and that the experiment can be replicated. What is being attempted is to derive some common characteristics of hypnotic depth which applies across individuals. To date, we do not know enough about altered states of consciousness to devise an experimental procedure which can do this adequately. This does not, however, mean that we have gained nothing from these tests. What has been established is that different tests can be successful whether in light, medium and deep hypnosis. This is simply because depth is not the only requirement for a suggestion to be successfully carried out. Expectation and general health, amongst other things, also influence the results.

The autohypnotist can derive from these tests what is usually considered a *typical* test of light, medium and deep hypnosis. They supply a basis on which to relate the subjective experience with other people's subjective experience – realizing that there are no hard and fast rules that one can apply. What must be avoided is the inclination to say, for example, that if you cannot attain partial amnesia that you are not in deep hypnosis. It may be that in your line of work not forgetting things is important, in which case this will also apply under hypnosis. Alternatively, some people may treat the suggestion to forget something as a command which they resent and, therefore, do not comply with it. What has been established from the verbal replies of many of these tests is that when a suggestion is not carried out in hypnosis, especially in medium and deep states, it is because the suggestion led to a conflict situation within the individual. The resolution of the conflict can be the situation of not carrying out the suggested instruction.

Linear or Non-linear Tests
The issue of depth arose very early in the history of hypnosis.

In Chapter 1 we mentioned Chastenet de Puységur who came across a somnambulist named Victor. A somnambulist is a person who enters the deepest form of hypnosis, which has as its main characteristic the fact that the person remembers nothing about the experience – unless instructed to do so. What this implies is that for a somnambulist, (left brain) consciousness is completely suspended. The scientific interest in a somnambulist arises from the fact that they can do a far greater range of 'unusual' things than the less deeply hypnotized person. In terms of simple test procedures, they define the limit of what a hypnotized person can do. From this arose a mistaken train of logical thought.

If you consider hypnosis *in a linear fashion*, as a continuum from being fully conscious to being in a somnambulistic state, as illustrated in Figure 5, then depth is also considered in a linear fashion. In other words, the closer you are to being a somnambulist the more deeply hypnotized you are. Or, alternatively, the closer you are to the waking conscious state the less deeply hypnotized you are. This view is implicit in both the Barber suggestibility scale and that presented by Davis and Husband – along with a number of others not discussed here.

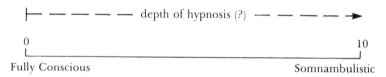

Figure 5

From this thought process the scientist would clearly like to obtain a scale which would measure how far a person is along this continuum. But what if hypnosis is *not* a linear progression from being fully conscious to being somnambulistic? Return to the analogy of the light bulbs that we discussed in Chapter 3. If the level of consciousness is characterized by a set of lights being on and off, then different states of consciousness are defined simply in terms of which lights are on and which are off. A look back at Table 3 will readily reveal that you cannot place states 1 to 8 along a straight line. It is true that state 1 can readily be identified as one extreme and state 8 as the other extreme, but the intermediate states cannot be placed in a linear fashion along a straight line. If this also applies to the state of hypnosis, which I believe is the case, then it is not sensible to construct a linear measure of hypnotic depth. By so doing, you impose on hypnosis a 'false' measure which then becomes part of the accepted notion of what hypnosis is.

In other words, suppose you construct a *linear* scale from 1 to 10 (fully conscious to the deepest form of hypnosis). Obviously with such a scale the closer a person is to 10 the more deeply hypnotized they will be classified – according to this scale of measurement. But if the scale is not linear then it is quite possible for a person lower down the scale to be more deeply hypnotized. Having said this, to prove this contention one would have to construct a non-linear measure of hypnosis and, having done so, re-classify individuals according to this non-linear measure and see if individuals are ranked differently. This is no easy task. The point of raising the issue is that if you believe a linear test is appropriate then you will not even look for a non-linear one. This should be kept in mind when considering the usefulness of the test procedures for measuring hypnotic depth.

Attitude to Adopt Towards the Depth of Hypnosis

Expectation and motivation play a major role in the achievement of hypnosis, therefore it is vital that you have the right attitude towards a deep hypnotic state. The first point is that it is not necessary always to go as deep as you possibly can. As we pointed out, the depth you require depends on what you want to achieve with the hypnosis. Second, if you want to go deep too earnestly then the principle of reverse effect (discussed in the next chapter) may take over and you will do quite the opposite. This is a common problem in many walks of life. You can want something too much. The most suitable attitude to take is to be indifferent about whether you go deeper or not: decide that you want to go deeper, but let circumstances dictate whether this is achieved. The point here is that you may undertake exercises deliberately to deepen the hypnosis, but what is being suggested is that you do not become concerned if you feel you are not being successful. Finally, do not analyse your reactions and sensations in order to 'see' if you are going deeper at the time of the hypnosis. This will simply activate the analytical faculties of the left brain and reduce your chance of going deeper.

For the autohypnotist what matters is *learning* to utilize the hypnotic state and *learning* to go deeper. Deepening the hypnotic state is a learning process which takes time. As in other walks of life, worrying about the lack of success only hinders the learning process. Wanting success too quickly without suitable preparation and learning can also lead to failure and frustration. Gradual practice at autohypnosis and applying techniques for deepening the state will eventually succeed. Readers interested in extending their range of techniques for deepening the hypnotic state may usefully consult Hartland,[18] Kroger[24] and Shone.[41]

6.
The Principles of Autohypnosis

To sum up the progress so far, we have discussed: the history of hypnosis, and particularly how this history bears on autohypnosis; the nervous system, and how this gives rise to positive hypnosis and negative hypnosis; consciousness and altered states of consciousness, arguing that hypnosis is just one of those states; the types of personalities which seem to be more likely to enter hypnosis; and, finally, aspects of the depth that a person can reach when entering hypnosis, most especially what this information gives to the person engaging in autohypnosis. In this chapter the intention is to pull together some of the strands that are outlined in earlier chapters which give rise to principles that underlie hypnosis in general, and autohypnosis in particular. These principles are usually given only cursory treatment in many works on hypnosis, but they deserve more attention. In giving them the status of a 'principle' they require some justification.

After discussing the three 'laws' of suggestion, we turn to some less familiar, and at the same time more problematic, principles. The principles which have been established are for hypnosis in general. What we wish to concentrate on in this chapter is how these principles need to be reformulated for the autohypnotist. Since, fundamentally, all hypnosis is autohypnosis, the principles should be the same. However, they have always been posed in such a way that heterohypnosis has been assumed to be the norm. To take just a single example at this point, *rapport* has always been stated as being important for hypnosis. But rapport is taken to be between the hypnotist and the subject. What, then, is the meaning of rapport in autohypnosis?

In discussing these principles in some detail, the intention is also to establish why it is more difficult for the autohypnotist to enter and deepen the hypnotic state than it is for a person to be hypnotized by someone else. But just because it is more difficult does not mean that the autohypnotist cannot gain anything from engaging in self-hypnosis; on the contrary, much can be gained. But what this gain is depends fundamentally on what you wish to do with the hypnotic state; that is to say, what suggestions you wish to give yourself when in self-hypnosis. Achieving autohypnosis is not an end in itself. What matters is how you utilize the state for your own well-being and your own self-development.

The Three Laws of Suggestion
At the heart of hypnosis is suggestion, and central to the workings of suggestion are three laws:

(1) The law of concentrated attention
(2) The law of reverse effect
(3) The law of dominant effect

In this section we shall discuss each of these in turn.

The law of concentrated attention
Hartland[18] puts it as follows: 'Whenever attention becomes concentrated upon an idea, that idea spontaneously tends to become realized.' (p.36) Let us break this principle down into component parts. The parts are: (a) concentrating one's attention, (b) focusing the attention on an idea, and (c) the result of carrying out (a) and (b).

The first part is rather ambiguous. Hartland goes on to say, 'it is the attention of the unconscious mind that we are trying to enlist'. But when you pay attention to something, this usually means that you bring it into *conscious* awareness. In fact, consciousness and attention are very closely associated – especially in cognitive psychology. What is in the forefront of your consciousness is precisely that to which you are paying attention. To clarify the point we need to distinguish two types of attention: *peripheral* attention and *focal* attention. You may be reading a book and concentrating on the story – you are focusing your attention on the story – but you can also be aware that someone has just entered the room – you are peripherally aware that someone has entered the room.[27] The principle is asserting that you must *focus* your attention on the idea, i.e., it must be in the forefront of your consciousness. To do this you must think about the idea; repeat any verbal suggestions that relate to it over and over again; see the idea from every point of view. In carrying out this operation you bring into the process not only your left hemisphere of the brain, but also your right. The fact that it is focally in your attention will mean that the idea will sink below your conscious mind and into your unconscious mind: it will pass from the left hemisphere of the brain into the right (and back again!).

The second part of the principle indicates that attention is focused on an *idea*. Why is this? An idea is not as well formulated as, say, an object. You can think about a chair by trying to see one that is familiar to you. In this case you are in fact retrieving a memory of a chair and bringing this into your consciousness. But you can also think about a chair in general, you can think about the 'idea of a chair': how different chairs look, the materials they are usually made of, the functions that they serve, etc. By concentrating on an idea, pictures and relationships form in the mind. These pictures and relationships are the essence of the right hemisphere of the brain. It is true that some of the relationships, such as logical relationships, are features of the left hemisphere of the brain; but in many respects ideas utilize both right and left hemispheres, with more emphasis on the right.

The third part of the principle says that the idea 'spontaneously tends to become realized'. No idea becomes *spontaneously* realized. What the principle is asserting is that if you focus on an idea sufficiently then that idea will give rise to changes in your behaviour or your way of thinking. If you focus on the idea of being happy, then you will become happy: the idea will become realized. But there is nothing spontaneous or inevitable about this. You are not guaranteed either to become happy or happy immediately. The reason is that this principle alone is not sufficient for an idea to become realized. It is necessary, but not sufficient, for the idea to become realized. All that can be asserted is that there will be a *tendency* for it to become realized – given that other factors are favourable.

What is not so clear in this principle is that when you focus your attention on an idea you bring into play both your conscious mind and your unconscious mind: both your left hemisphere and your right hemisphere of the brain. Even the scientist does this when grappling with a problem. The problem can be in the focus of attention but not yet solved. He may then, as Poincaré did when trying to solve a mathematical problem, forget about it for a time and suddenly the solution comes – in Poincaré's case it was just as he was about to step on a bus![31] What appears to have happened is that the problem was processed further by the unconscious mind and once solved was thrown into conscious awareness. The solution could not have been derived without the initial focus and concentration. The idea had to be thought out in all its aspects first. The point about this example is that it is in relation to a mathematical idea. When the idea is about behaviour the likelihood of the idea becoming realized is greater. The reason for this we shall discuss later, but for the moment we can say it is because of the emotional content involved.

The law of reverse effect
This law states that: the harder one tries to do something, the less successful one is likely to be. The most common everyday examples of this principle in operation are: (a) trying hard to get to sleep and being totally unsuccessful; (b) trying hard to remember a name, equally without success; and (c) trying hard to play a good game of golf or tennis, and making things worse. It is often characteristic of dieters. The harder they try to diet the more they think about food, and very soon the more they eat! Why it is that trying *too* hard creates a reverse effect while trying, but not too hard, does not, is not known. However, it probably has something to do with how the two halves of the brain interrelate with one another. 'Trying too hard' implies that a conscious act is involved. One is consciously trying to get to sleep; one is trying consciously to remember a name; one is trying consciously to play tennis well. It is as if the conscious trying is interfering with the 'natural' process. It is reasonable to conjecture that what is taking place is a situation where the conscious trying is interfering with the unconscious workings of the right hemisphere of the brain. It is very much as if you are happily doing a job and then someone comes along and tries to tell you, very forcefully, how to do it better. Would you do it better? Probably not.

This appears to be one of the major reasons why some people do not enter hypnosis although they may want to. They may want to so much that they try too hard. The trying too hard simply makes things worse and they do not enter hypnosis. Of course, this is not because they are not hypnotizable, but rather because they are trying too hard and interfering with the brain's natural workings, which will quite naturally allow a person to enter into a state of hypnosis. This is especially true of a person engaging in autohypnosis.

How one determines to distinguish between concentrated attention and trying too hard is difficult to describe. But once a person has entered hypnosis on previous occasions and fails to do so on a subsequent occasion, it becomes possible to recognize when the principle of reverse effect appears to be the cause. When this happens, either you stop trying too hard, or else you abandon the attempt on this occasion.

Before leaving the principle of reverse effect, it is worth mentioning the fact that it is possible for someone to take advantage of this 'law'. Take, for example, an analyst who is attempting to get someone into a hypnotic state. The usual induction procedure is to attempt to get them to close their eyes; suggestions about tiredness and heaviness of the eyelids are usually employed to do this. But suppose the law of reverse effect is operating and that the more you suggest to a person that they are tired, etc., the less tired they seem to become. You could, then, reverse the suggestions! You could, for example, suggest that they try to keep their eyes open, and that whatever suggestions are made their eyes will remain open. If the principle is truly operating then soon they will do the opposite and close their eyes! It is also very commonly utilized within the induction process. It is common to suggest to someone, or to oneself, that an arm is getting stiff and rigid and that when the person tries to bend it then it will become even more stiff and rigid. In other words, the act of trying to bend it makes it even straighter and stiffer!

The law of dominant effect
This principle states that: a strong emotion will tend to replace a weaker one. This principle means that if a strong emotion is attached to a suggestion then it is more likely that the suggestion will be effective. If we take two emotions, such as pleasure and a sense of danger, then the second is the stronger of the two. If a person is having a pleasurable emotion and danger becomes imminent, then the emotion of danger will displace the emotion of pleasure. To give a very simple

illustration of this 'law', suppose that someone suggested to you that you were to relax. You may, in fact, relax. But if someone were to massage you *and* suggest to you that you were to relax, then you almost certainly would. The strongest emotion here is that of sensation and comfort.

There are two reasons why attaching emotion to a suggestion will make it more effective. First, an emotion is felt immediately. There is no such thing as an emotion in the future, or a delayed emotion. Because of this, the suggestion to which it is attached also tends to be effective immediately. Second, an emotion involves the right hemisphere of the brain and, because of this, the suggestion gets more quickly assimilated by the unconscious mind. It is as if the link with the emotion allows the suggestion to pass from the left hemisphere of the brain and into the right hemisphere quickly and with ease.

Because of the importance played by emotion in suggestions it is worth commenting on it further. Emotion has two facets: first, physiological – the body changes that occur when an emotion is felt; and second, behavioural – the changes in behaviour that are undertaken when an emotion is felt. Both of these facets are utilized in hypnotherapy – and can also be

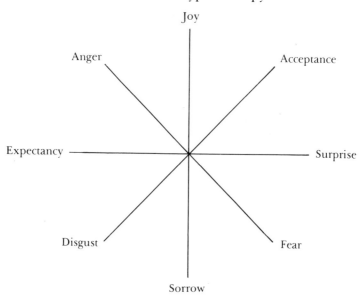

Figure 6
Plutchik's circular ordering of eight primary emotions

utilized by the autohypnotist. When you become angry your heart starts to beat faster, your breathing becomes deeper and quicker, and you become flushed. One way to self-improvement is to 'observe' how your body responds to different emotions. But it is not so easy to bring about these emotions. One method is by imagery, as outlined in the author's *Creative Visualization*.[42] But what are the emotions to be elicited? We can use Plutchik's classification and distinguish eight primary emotions set out in a circular dimension, as shown in Figure 6, with similar emotions being next to each other.[36]

Secondary emotions, according to Plutchik, can be represented by a combination of these primary emotions. Thus, shame is the combination of fear and disgust; love the combination of joy and acceptance. Of course, this is just one approach to the nature of emotion, and there are many others. From our present point of view what matters is that you have become acquainted with your emotions. Once you have become acquainted with them, then it is possible to control them – if that is what you wish to do.

Principles of Hypnosis

The principles of hypnosis follow quite naturally from the three 'laws' of suggestion outlined in the previous section. Three principles have been stated by Harland:[18]

> 1. You should always couple an effect that you want to produce with one that the subject is actually experiencing at the moment. . . .
> 2. It is always much easier to secure the acceptance of a positive suggestion than a purely negative one. . . .
> 3. It is sometimes easier to secure the acceptance of a suggestion if it is coupled with an appropriate emotion.

The first principle is attempting to relate suggestion to an action. It is important to realize that an action causes an immediate response from the body and so if a suggestion is coupled with something that the subject is actually experiencing at the time, then it is more likely to be acted upon. To take a simple illustration, if you were suggesting to someone under hypnosis that their hand was becoming numb, then it is useful to stroke the hand at the same time. The sensation of touch directs the subject's attention to the hand and gives immediate body reponses. In autohypnosis it is not always so easy to carry out this coupling because it requires too much conscious effort. However, there are some simple actions. For instance, rather than just suggesting to yourself that you are getting deeper and deeper, it is possible to have your arms circling around one another and to suggest that as you go deeper and deeper then the circling will become quicker and quicker, (Shone,[41] Chapter 3). What this, and other similar actions, does is to establish a feedback mechanism. The circling gives some indication of the deepening. It is as if success is being registered by the circling action. As some success is being registered, so expectation of further success is enhanced and doubt reduced.

The second principle is somewhat ambiguous. It means that a suggestion under hypnosis should be indicating a positive response rather than a negative one. To illustrate this let us suppose that you are attempting to get rid of a headache. A negative response is to suggest that the headache will disappear – either immediately or in so many minutes. A positive suggestion is one which displaces the feelings associated with a headache and, if strong enough, will replace it. Thus, suggestions could go along the lines of feeling warm, secure, free from tension etc., and that as these feelings occur the individual will feel less and less the pain of the headache. One way to think of this principle is make suggestions in terms of adding rather than subtracting! It is ambiguous only to the extent that it would suggest that positive suggestions are more powerful than negative ones. This is not necessarily true. Negative suggestions, coupled usually with the imagination, are very powerful. What the principle is saying is that to overcome an already negative situation, you require a powerful positive force. The more powerful the negative situation, the more powerful needs to be the positive force.

The third principle has been highlighted throughout this book. Emotion is immediate. If a suggestion can be coupled with the *appropriate* emotion then it is more likely to be successful. Emphasis is undoubtedly on the 'appropriateness' of the associated emotion. Suppose, for example, you are obese and are wanting to lose weight. You may be carrying out suggestions to the effect that you will lose weight or that you will eat less. If the suggestions were simply verbal, and nothing more, then it is unlikely that they will be successful. What is required is some form of emotion. It is usual in situations of this kind to employ aversion therapy. The emotion called on is either nausea (possibly in the form of vomiting) or revulsion and disgust – revulsion at the sight of someone obese and disgust at oneself for becoming obese. Without such emotion the loss of weight cannot be achieved. There is no point in giving yourself suggestions to the effect of losing weight *and simultaneously* not having an aversion to being and looking fat, (see Hariman,[17] Chapter 6.)

These three principles apply to hypnosis in general, but they equally apply to anyone engaging in autohypnosis. The difficulty encountered by the autohypnotist is coupling the suggestions with actions and emotions without disturbing the hypnotic state. This becomes easier with practice. But one useful technique to develop is carrying out suggestions with the eyes open. We shall discuss this in more detail in the final chapter.

Other Principles

So far we have concentrated on the major principles of suggestion and hypnosis. There are also a number of principles which apply more specifically to given situations. We need only list these because they are self-explanatory. They are:

(1) When giving suggestions try to picture appropriate situations in relation to the suggestions – these should be vivid and contain emotion.

(2) Always enter hypnosis with an expectation of success.

(3) Always make suggestions simple, clear and unambiguous.

(4) Always pause between suggestions relating to different ideas.

(5) Suggestions should be repeated slowly and rhythmically, even during autohypnosis.

(6) Suggestions concerned with changes in your actions or behaviour should be left until towards the end of the hypnotic session (or when you consider you are at the deepest point).

(7) Suggestions should not go against your moral code.

Rapport and Autohypnosis

It is worth concluding this chapter with a discussion of rapport in relation to autohypnosis. Hartland[18] defines rapport as follows,

. . . a state of affinity existing between subject and hypnotist and is present at the very onset of hypnosis. It is of such a nature that it tends to prevent the subject from responding to any stimuli other than those arising from the hypnotist himself unless he instructs the subject otherwise. (p.163)

He goes on to say,

> Essentially, rapport seems to be a kind of mental sympathy which gradually develops through repetition into a state of exaggerated belief and trust on the part of the subject which often leads to a form of emotional attachment between subject and hypnotist. (p.164)

It is clear that rapport is a concept usually attached to heterohypnosis: it refers to a relationship between subject and hypnotist. The question I wish to raise here is whether rapport can occur in autohypnosis. If this is so, what form does it take?

Let me state emphatically that rapport can exist in the autohypnotic state. In justifying this, and explaining the form it takes, it is useful to break down the concept of rapport into three component parts.

> (1) It is a relationship between subject and the hypnotist.
> (2) 'It is of such a nature that it tends to prevent the subject from responding to any stimuli other than those arising from the hypnotist himself.'
> (3) It is an 'exaggerated belief and trust on the part of the subject'.

When engaging in self-hypnosis one utilizes the fact that each of us has many selves – a point we discussed in Chapter 3. Once we accept that we have many selves then it is not too difficult to argue that one self is the person being hypnotized, while another self is the hypnotist. Thus rapport is now a relationship between two selves which exist in the one person. Rapport is easier in heterohypnosis only to the extent that the subject and the hypnotist appear as definitely separate individuals. But there is nothing inherently different about rapport between two selves in the same individual. What is difficult is 'seeing' the two selves as distinct persons. This is not as difficult as it may sound. Occasionally we all find that we are observing ourselves doing a task; it is a situation of self-observation. Who is the one doing the task and who is the one looking on? In this situation there are two selves: the self doing the task and the self looking on. It is this separation of selves which is required in autohypnosis and which allows rapport to exist.

The second aspect is in paying attention to nothing other than what the hypnotist is saying. In this respect the subject-self is paying attention to nothing other than the hypnotist-self. Once the two selves have been clearly delineated in the mind, this is not at all difficult to do. It is no more difficult than listening to a hypnotist who appears to be another person.

Furthermore, the third aspect is also capable of being established, namely, exaggerated trust and belief. Here is a possible stumbling block. What is clearly required is the subject-self having trust and belief in the hypnotist-self.

How does the autohypnotist go about doing this? The most obvious way is for an individual to learn all about the hypnotic state and, just as importantly, practise self hypnosis. With practice comes ability and, through ability, confidence. Reading about hypnosis is not sufficient – you cannot climb a mountain simply by reading how! Practice without knowledge is also not sufficient – climbing a mountain without knowing its difficulties and without knowing what is the right equipment to take is silly and possibly dangerous! The most essential feature, however, is the recognition and belief in the existence of many selves. Without this the autohypnotist cannot establish rapport and cannot derive *full* advantage from the hypnotic state, although some advantage is still possible.

7.
Relationship With Other Subjects

In this chapter the aim is to discuss autohypnosis and its relationship with other subjects, such as biofeedback, yoga, meditation, religion and faith-healing. There is no intention to discuss these topics in detail, or as topics in their own right, but rather to concentrate on those aspects which overlap with autohypnosis – or even to discuss whether there exists any overlap with autohypnosis.

The discussion will be aided by stating from the outset the author's particular point of view. This can best be seen in terms of Figure 7. It will be noted from this figure that

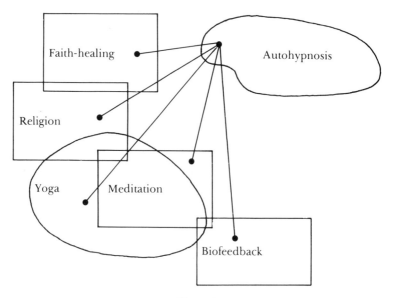

Figure 7

hypnosis is seen as being separate from, but having similarities with, each of religion, faith-healing, yoga, meditation and biofeedback. It is also seen from Figure 7 that the topics themselves overlap one another. In this chapter there is no intention to discuss the overlap between each of these subject areas, but rather to concentrate on the differences and similarities between autohypnosis and these topics.

The discussion will inevitably be fuzzy because the boundaries between these subjects are unclear, and certainly the connection and overlap between them is unclear. Each subject has its exponents and, one might say, its gurus. But any reading of the literature will show that they do have a number of similarities as well as a number of differences. The simplest approach to this vast topic is to take each subject in turn, and then finish by commenting on some similarities between all the connections.

Biofeedback

Biofeedback was to a large extent pioneered by Dr Elmer Green of the Manninger Foundation. It is a behavioural technique which uses instruments to help individuals become aware of their biological condition, most especially their autonomic processes. An individual is linked up to a machine which records body changes, such as brainwave patterns (by using an electroencephalograph EEG), muscle tension (by using an electromyograph EMG), or skin resistance (by using a galvanic skin response meter GSR). The individual is given instructions on relaxing or attempting to change some autonomic response, such as the heartbeat. Any changes that occur are monitored by the machine and (usually) amplified so that the individual may see or hear any changes that are occurring. By taking note of such changes the individual can increase the frequency of 'correct' responses. The process is illustrated in Figure 8 (page 96).

The eventual aim of biofeedback, as Figure 8 makes clear on the right-hand side, is to eliminate the machine altogether. Individuals, once they become aware of their autonomic responses, can change them, and monitor them, by self-observation. The machines are purely a means of learning the technique.

The early use of biofeedback was in alleviating symptoms, such as chronic headache. It will be useful in making our comparison to outline exactly how this was accomplished.

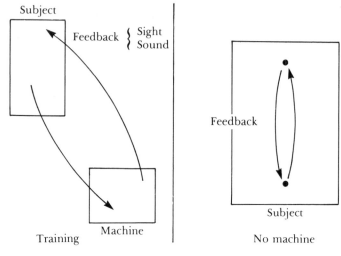

Figure 8

Wallace and Fisher[48] explain it as follows:

> In this process the trainee is made conscious of the activity level of a small pair of muscles located near the centre of the forehead. These are the fontalis muscles. The subject's task is to reduce the activity level, and thus the tension, of these muscles. The rationale underlying this approach is that, by relaxing this muscle pair, biofeedback training will generalize the relaxation to the untrained muscles, and they, too, will show a decrease in tension. (p.76)

What is clear from this commentary is that the individual is being trained to concentrate on some area of the body, with the help of a machine. However, the machine only aids in directing attention to the right part of the autonomic nervous system. The mind must do the rest.

This is the similarity with hypnosis. As in autohypnosis, there is directed attention on a stimulus which brings about an altered state of consciousness. Where it differs from hypnosis is in the fact that it provides the individual with an audible or visible means of perceiving quickly any physiological change taking place in the body. Of course, once the machine becomes redundant, once the person knows subjectively how to monitor their bodily changes, then everything becomes internalized. When this happens, the similarity with auto-hypnosis (and other altered states of consciousness) becomes greater.

What is clear, however, is that there is no machine which can monitor hypnosis. There is no way to obtain feedback from a machine about whether an individual is entering hypnosis and is, for example, going deeper. The reason is that there is no obvious correlation between hypnosis and changes taking place in a person's physiology. Hence, there is nothing, in fact, to monitor! In biofeedback, on the other hand, there is a definite physiological response being monitored – whether this be heartbeat or skin resistance. Any gadgets that do exist in connection with hypnosis are purely aids for entering the hypnotic state but do not monitor it.

It is possible to use biofeedback machines on someone entering hypnosis, but they only register that *something* is happening. In fact, all the machine is registering is that the individual is becoming relaxed as he enters hypnosis. There is nothing unique to hypnosis which is being monitored or measured. The point has been put very well by Blythe,[6]

> However, none of the biofeedback instruments in themselves produce any form of hypnosis. I have given the GSR [Galvanic skin response meter] to many clients who have had difficulty in letting go of their need for self-control, in order that they can learn to adopt a passive, 'let it happen', mental attitude. (p.154)

As this quotation makes clear, biofeedback machines can be used in *conjunction with* hypnosis, but biofeedback and hypnosis are fundamentally different things.

Yoga and Meditation

It has often been claimed that there are many similarities between yoga and autohypnosis or between meditation and autohypnosis. To begin with we have placed yoga and meditation together. Yoga is broader than meditation, but utilizes meditation as one of its main planks. It is possible to argue that there are many forms of meditation – such as Zen, Yoga, TM and sufism – and that they differ only in the form which meditation takes. Whichever form, however, they all involve a series of repetitive exercises: on a mantram (a word or phrase), as in Zen and yoga; on a mandala (a visual object), as in yoga; on a tratakam (a steady gaze, for example at a candle flame), as in yoga; or on a madra (a repetitive physical movement of the body), as in yoga and sufism.

In the West most attention has been concentrated on

transcendental meditation, TM. The reason for this is not hard to understand. Zen and yoga, for example, take years to master, while TM takes only hours to master. Furthermore, with TM there is no requirement to accept any underlying religion or philosophy or to change one's lifestyle, no need to change one's diet or to engage in contorting exercises, there is no need to retreat from the world of reality into a world of isolation or spirituality.

The interest in TM has meant that more research has been undertaken into this than into any other form of meditation. The benefits which are associated with TM are:

– increased energy for living and working
– a new inner mental tranquillity
– less physical and mental tension
– loss of desire for drugs
– restoration of sleeping patterns and less sleep
– a better ability to cope with adverse situations

But these are all a result of relaxation and a reduction in tension. The only benefit in this list which is particular to meditation (and not only TM) is a new inner mental tranquillity. In so far as autohypnosis brings about relaxation and reduced tension, it also produces these same benefits. Even where it is claimed that in meditation, in contrast to hypnosis, metabolic changes occur faster and that there is deeper relaxation, this has not really been proven. It could simply be that the subjects chosen are more adept at entering meditation than they are at entering a state of hypnosis. Certainly, autohypnosis is harder to learn than transcendental meditation. It has also been claimed that meditators require less sleep – four hours rather than the usual eight hours. But again, the reduction in sleep requirement is not unique to TM but arises from the relaxation and reduced tension. This should not be surprising. One of the reasons why we sleep is so that the body can relax and have relief from tension. Whatever, therefore, gives rise to relaxation and reduced tension will also mean that the individual concerned will require less sleep.

The similarity between meditation and hypnosis has been aptly put by Wallace and Fisher:[48]

> As we mentioned, many forms of meditation are similar to hypnosis. In both situations, an individual must concentrate on a

stimulus, thereby blocking external interference. In hypnosis, the stimulus to which an individual attends is typically the voice of the hypnotist. In meditation, the stimulus is either a visual object of regard, a physical motion of the body, or a chant.

However, it is possible to induce an altered state of consciousness by hypnotizing oneself. This process is called *autohypnosis* or self-hypnosis. The individual concentrates on a stimulus of his or her own choosing, and the net result is a very relaxed feeling. In fact, the behavior exhibited in self-hypnosis approximates the behavior observed in meditation, especially the Zen variety of meditation. Also, as in self-hypnosis, meditation is a procedure one must learn. The ability to hypnotize oneself or to meditate does not come either instantly or easily. One must practice for periods of time and on many occasions before one can concentrate effectively on a situation while attenuating potential sources of disturbance. Typically, initial attempts at self-hypnosis or meditation meet with failure because (1) it is difficult to concentrate on only one thing for a period of time, and (2) most people have never had to do this or anything like it before. (pp.84-5)

The emphasis on relaxation in meditation is obvious and is one of the primary benefits from undertaking meditation. But, as the quotation makes clear, the same benefit can be achieved by autohypnosis. What meditation can provide, which is not necessarily the case with autohypnosis, is an inner mental tranquillity. One of the differences between hypnosis and meditation that is sometimes put forward is that the former can help resolve unconscious problems which arise from the past and which meditation cannot do. But this confuses hypnosis with hypnotherapy. It is the therapy which uncovers the unresolved conflicts not the hypnosis. The conclusion which can be drawn is that meditation is not the best means of bringing to the surface such unresolved conflicts. But it is probably better for coping with everyday tension.

When a person asks, 'What is the difference between meditation and autohypnosis?' they are usually concerned with what course of action they should take, and not because of any intellectual curiosity. Should I learn how to meditate, or should I learn self-hypnosis? They seek the best method. But often people are unclear about what it is that they want from these techniques. Each is a means to an end and not an end in itself. One learns self-hypnosis in order to achieve relaxation, relief from pain or whatever. One learns meditation in order to achieve relaxation and an inner mental tranquillity. Which should be learned (and may include both) depends on one's ultimate objective.

Religion and Faith-healing

Religion and faith-healing have in common belief and conviction. But it is, to a large extent, these factors which are also important in hypnosis. A person cannot enter hypnosis if he believes that he cannot; nor can he enter hypnosis if he has no desire to do so. Of course, religion is much more than just faith and conviction. But from our present point of view, what matters is that religion (all religions) and faith-healing utilize the power of suggestion – whether consciously or unconsciously.

Kroger[24] points out the similarity as follows:

> Prayer, particularly in the Jewish and the Christian religions, has many similarities to hypnotic induction. There is the regular cadence and intonation in the prayers (chanting), a relaxing environment, and the fixation of attention on the altar or religious leader. In Judaism, there is a rhythmic rocking of the body back and forth in time to the chanting which is hypnagogic. Finally, the contemplation, the meditation, and the self-absorption character-istic of prayer are almost identical with autohypnosis. (p.125)

In many religious practices there are clear attempts to place the individual into a frame of mind so that they will accept certain teachings, certain ideas. These are not logical ideas and cannot be absorbed in a logical manner. Consequently, an alternative method must be sought. If one thinks about religious practices objectively, it will be realized that they appeal to the right brain and not the left. The cross, the star of David, the rosaries, the mandala, all are a means of focusing attention on a thought. The Church may have doubts about hypnosis but they put many of its principles into practice!

Faith-healing is largely based on belief and conviction: both from the person doing the healing and the person being healed. The success of faith-healing over, say, autohypnosis, is in the individual's conviction that *their* illness cannot be cured by self-hypnosis, but can be cured by a certain faith-healer. It is this conviction and belief which is the essential ingredient, and it is this which is the same ingredient for autohypnosis.

Conclusion

Hypnosis, biofeedback, meditation, yoga, religion and faith-healing, all have in common that their success depends on appealing to the right brain. The connection between auto-hypnosis and these other topics is in terms of the techniques that they employ – whether it is a technique of contemplation or a technique to alter the autonomic nervous system. In particular, meditation and autohypnosis, but not biofeedback, can be regarded as a slow, cumulative and long-term procedure for producing an altered state of consciousness. Biofeedback can be considered as a short-term device to teach people how to do this, and to demonstrate to them that it is possible to achieve an altered state of consciousness. You may consider yourself relaxed, for example, but how do you know this? You may be sitting or lying in what to you appears a relaxed position, but you may not be so. A biofeedback machine can inform you whether you are or not. Once you have learned to become relaxed you can then discard the machine.

The consideration of meditation and religious practices indicates that the concentration on an object, a phrase, a thought or a body movement, is a means of altering one's state of consciousness. But even these will be unsuccessful without faith and belief.

8.
Advanced Techniques

The aim of this brief chapter is to provide techniques for improving autohypnosis *with the eyes open*. It will be recalled from Chapter 2 on the nervous system that a considerable amount of sensory information enters through the eyes. Because of this, the sooner the eyes are closed the easier it is to enter a hypnotic state. Studies have certainly shown that with the eyes closed and in a relaxed state – not necessarily a hypnotic state – the brain produces alpha rhythms. When the eyes are opened these rhythms tend to disappear, and when the eyes are closed once again, the alpha rhythms re-emerge. But hypnosis and alpha rhythms are not the same thing. Furthermore, relaxation is only a prerequisite for entering hypnosis. Research has also shown that there is no obvious correlation between hypnosis and physiological responses – as there is, for example, in biofeedback or meditation. In addition, the research we have presented in this book indicates that the individual has far more control over his states of consciousness than has been formerly realized.

From these observations we can draw an important conclusion. Although closing the eyes and relaxing is important for entering a hypnotic state, it does not follow that opening the eyes will *automatically* terminate the hypnotic state. Many people come out of hypnosis when they open their eyes for the simple reason that they believe they are only 'hypnotized' when they have their eyes closed and cannot be 'hypnotized' when their eyes are open. But even if a person does not hold such an erroneous view, it does not mean that it is as easy to maintain hypnosis while the eyes are open. This is a technique which must be learnt. Before mentioning any techniques, however, the obvious question which arises is, 'Why should I want to learn autohypnosis with my eyes open?' In answer to this question we return to a point made frequently throughout this book. There is nothing intrinsically useful in hypnosis. The usefulness depends on what you wish to do with the hypnosis.

We shall not discuss techniques here, largely because there are a number of books available which discuss them, and some of these can be found in the references. However, four broad areas stand out.

1. Relaxation
2. Behaviour modification
3. Illness
4. Self-improvement.

If the reader does not consider these four areas, taken as a whole, as important then learning autohypnosis, with or without the eyes open, will not be considered worthwhile. If you do consider them important and wish to do something about any, or all, of them, then learning autohypnosis is worthwhile. Furthermore, like any learned technique, you can do more with it the more proficient you are. The technique we are about to discuss is just an enhancement of those techniques discussed in the author's *Autohypnosis*.[41]

Autohypnosis With The Eyes Open

Because hypnosis is a learning process the aim is to learn to preserve the autohypnotic state while the eyes are open. The first essential requirement is that you believe this is possible. Hopefully, the arguments we have presented in this book will provide a basis for such a belief. Second, it is assumed that you know how to enter, deepen and come out of hypnosis; furthermore, that you have become reasonably proficient at this.

The first part of the technique is to practise retaining the hypnotic state with your eyes open. To do this it is useful, and certainly helps the hypnosis, if you can also achieve some feedback (just as in biofeedback). This can be accomplished by using a mirror – the bigger the mirror the better. Whether you are initially lying down or seated in a chair, the aim is to achieve as deep a hypnotic state as you can and then give yourself instructions for opening your eyes. At this stage you should either be in a chair in front of the mirror, or have a chair ready in front of the mirror. In these instructions we shall suppose you are already in a chair facing the mirror. The instructions can run along the following lines:

> In a moment I am going to open my eyes slowly. I will remain in hypnosis with no difficulty at all. I will remain calm and relaxed and in a deep hypnotic state, even though my eyes are open. In fact, with every breath I take, my hypnosis will go deeper and deeper, even though my eyes are open. On the count of three I will open my eyes and remain in a deep hypnotic state. One. . . Two. . . Three.

These instructions are very simple. They should be repeated a few times and, if you come out of the hypnotic state on opening your eyes, then simply keep practising.

If you are in hypnosis you will not only feel it, but now that you are looking into a mirror you will see the very relaxed facial expression and drooped shoulders. Not only will you feel your body heavy, but you will not want to move it. Your eyes may roam over your body very slowly and you may even just look at certain parts of your body. These observations provide important feedback to the brain, indicating that you are different. Your expression will be one of a fixed glare – unless you give yourself instructions to the contrary (which we shall deal with in a moment).

During some early practice sessions it is useful to go over simple exercises and not only feel yourself responding, but also see yourself responding. For example, give yourself suggestions that you will try to get out of the chair but will have great difficulty in doing so. The fact that you can *see* the difficulty as well as *feel* the difficulty makes the suggestion stronger. The point about going over some standard and simple exercises is so that you can get used to *seeing* how your body responds to the suggestions. Take another very simple example, suppose you suggest to yourself that on a given instruction you will have a tremendous urge to laugh and that with each moment that passes, until you give instructions to the contrary, this urge to laugh will get greater and greater. As you begin to respond to the suggestion the fact that you can *see* the response reinforces it much more strongly than simply feeling it. This is because we depend so much on our sight, that seeing our facial expression change indicates a positive response and an expectation of success – all essential ingredients for hypnosis.

The point of these early exercises is simply to become used to the idea of giving yourself suggestions with your eyes open and noting the responses. Once this has been accomplished you can progress onto further exercises, most notably changes in feelings about the body. We pointed out that hypnosis does not have any obvious physiological correlates, this is because you can control your body to the extent that it 'behaves' as it would in a normal waking state. Let us take a very simple example. Suppose you were to give yourself the suggestions that you will feel very physical, that you will note all the muscles of your body, that you will feel a tremendous power surging through your body. With such suggestions you would begin to feel these feelings. Not only that, you would begin to change your body posture in the light of images that you would be forming in the mind. The stronger the images, the more you are likely to change your body, and the more you *see* the change in your body posture the easier it will be to enhance the feeling. This is no more than the biofeedback method we discussed in Chapter 7. The only difference is that the 'machine' is simply a mirror.

At this early stage the aim is to practise eliciting various responses – sadness, happiness, excitement, and so on. As you practise these you become more adept at creating any type of person you wish. Sometimes the hypnosis will lighten but on other occasions it may deepen. Why some of the suggestions lead to a lightening of hypnosis and others to a deepening of the hypnotic state probably has to do with the subjective or objective nature of the suggestions – as we discussed in terms of Huxley's experiences. Although these suggestions in and of themselves serve no purpose, it is important that you practise eliciting various responses so that you can achieve a full range of changes. Such practice will also give you some idea of the full potential of autohypnosis when the eyes are open.

In the early practice sessions you will probably only retain hypnosis with the eyes open for short periods of time – about ten minutes – but with practice this will lengthen. This is not surprising. When the eyes are open you very soon begin to respond the way you always have in a normal waking state, so you very soon slip into this mode of consciousness. The whole point of practising is so that you can prevent this from happening.

Once you have achieved some success in front of the

mirror, you can go beyond this. As in biofeedback, where the aim is eventually to dispense with the machine and achieve alterations of the autonomic nervous system unaided by the machine, so you eventually want to be able to achieve autohypnosis with the eyes open when you are not in front of a mirror. Now that you can retain hypnosis with the eyes open you can incorporate in your suggestions three possible visual aids: photographs, pictures and drawings. How these are used depends on your ultimate objective. If, for example, you are trying to get over some illness then you can have a photograph of yourself when you were well, or a picture of another healthy person. Alternatively, you can draw your illness and draw how you can rid yourself of it. The possibilities for altering behaviour and self-improvement are endless. They depend on how you wish to improve. However, I am not suggesting for a moment that these will be easily accomplished. What I am saying is that the present technique is *one* means of doing this.

Ultimately what is being suggested is that you can achieve a flexible and malleable behaviour which is more under your conscious control than it had been before you engaged in autohypnosis. It does not, of course, mean that you will not respond to many unconscious forces. What it will mean is that you are more consciously aware of what you are doing and why.

Furthermore, the ability to achieve self-hypnosis at any time and in any place, with or without your eyes open, means that you can always receive the benefits of light hypnosis which involves relaxation. In all the writings on hypnosis there is nothing that would indicate that you cannot enter hypnosis while standing at a bus stop and appearing, to all other people, as 'normal' while being, in fact, in a state of autohypnosis.

The idea that you must be lying down, with your eyes closed and unconscious, has been such a strong suggestion that it has blinded people as to what hypnosis is and the range of conditions under which it can occur. It is hoped that this book will give some idea of the full potential of autohypnosis.

References

1. Arluck, E. W., *Hypnoanalysis: A Case Study* (Random House, 1964)
2. Barber, T. X., Spanos, N. P. and Chaves, J. F., *Hypnotism, Imagination and Human Potentialities* (Pergamon Press, 1974)
3. Baudouin, C., *Suggestion and Autosuggestion* (Dodd, Mead & Co., 1922)
4. Berne. E., *Games People Play* (Penguin, 1964)
5. Blakeslee, T. R., *The Right Brain* (Macmillan, 1980)
6. Blythe, P., *Self-Hypnotism* (Arthur Barker Limited, 1976)
7. Cotman, C. W. and McGaugh, J. L. *Behavioral Neuroscience* (Academic Press, 1980)
8. Davis, L. W. and Husband, R. W. 'A Study of Hypnotic Susceptibility in Relation to Personality Traits' in L. Kuhn and S. Russo (eds.), *Modern Hypnosis* (Wilshire Book Company, 1958)
9. Eccles, J. C., *The Understanding of the Brain* (McGraw-Hill, 1973)
10. Edmunds, S., *Hypnotism and Psychic Phenomena* (Wilshire Book Company, 1961)
11. Evans, F. J., 'Hypnosis and Sleep: Techniques for Exploring Cognitive Activity During Sleep' reprinted in E. Fromm and R. E. Shor (eds.,) *Hypnosis: Research Developments and Perspectives* (Paul Elek [Scientific Books] Ltd, 1972)
12. Erickson, H., 'A Special Inquiry with Aldous Huxley into the Nature and Character of Various States of Consciousness' reprinted in C. T. Tart (ed.), *Altered States of Consciousness* (Doubleday & Company, Inc., 1969)
13. Eysenck, H. J., *You and Neurosis* (Fontana, 1977)
14. Ferguson, M., *The Aquarian Conspiracy* (Granada, 1980)
15. Fisher, C., 'Hypnosis in Treatment of Neuroses Due to War and Other Causes' in L. Kuhn and S. Russo (eds.), *Modern Hypnosis* (Wilshire Book Company, 1958)
16. Guyton, A. C., *Structure and Function of the Nervous System* (W. B. Saunders Company, 1972)
17. Hariman, Jusuf, *How to Use the Power of Self-Hypnosis* (Thorsons, 1981)

18. Hartland, J., *Medical and Dental Hypnosis and its Clinical Applications* (Balliere Tindall, 1966)
19. Helleberg, M. M., *Beyond TM* (Paulist Press, 1980)
20. Hilgard, E. R., *The Experience of Hypnosis* (Harcourt Brace Jovanovich,1968)
21. Hilgard, J. R., *Personality and Hypnosis* (The University of Chicago Press, 1970)
22. Hull, C. L., *Hypnosis and Suggestibility* (Appleton-Century-Crofts, 1933)
23. Jaynes, J., *The Origin of Consciousness in the Breakdown of the Bicameral Mind* (Penguin, 1976)
24. Kroger, W. S., *Clinical and Experimental Hypnosis* (J. B. Lippincott Company, 1963)
25. Ludwig, A. M., 'Altered States of Consciousness' reprinted in C. T. Tart (ed.) *Altered States of Consciousness* (Doubleday & Company, Inc., 1969)
26. Luria, A. R., *The Working Brain* (Penguin, 1933)
27. Lloyd, P. and Mayers, A., *Introduction to Psychology* (Penguin, 1984)
28. Maltz, M., *Psycho-Cybernetics* (Wilshire Book Co., 1960)
29. Marcuse, F. L., *Hypnosis: Fact and Fiction* (Penguin, 1959)
30. Masters, R. E. L. and Houston, J., *Mind Games* (Turnstone Press, 1973)
31. Moss, P. and Keeton, J., *Encounters with the Past* (Penguin, 1979)
32. New Scientist, 'Hypnosis relies on left-brain dominance' *New Scientist* (2 August, 1984)
33. Ornstein, R. E., *The Psychology of Consciousness* (Penguin, 1977)
34. Poincaré, H., 'Mathematical Creation' *Scientific America* (August 1948)
35. Popper, K. P., and Eccles, J. C., *The Self and Its Brain* (Routledge & Kegan Paul, 1983)
36. Plutchik, R., *Emotion: A Psychoevolutionary Synthesis* (Harper and Row, 1980)
37. Ropp, R. S. de, *The Master Game* (Picador, 1974)
38. Russell, P., *The Brain Book* (Routledge & Kegan Paul, 1979)
39. Saparina, Y., *Cybernetics Within Us* (Wilshire Book Co., 1967)
40. Sarbin, T. R., 'Contributions to role-taking theory: I. Hypnotic Behavior' *Psychological Review, Vol. 57* (1950)
41. Shone, R., *Autohypnosis* (Thorsons, 1982)
42. Shone, R., *Creative Visualization* (Thorsons, 1984)
43. Shor, R. E., 'Hypnosis and the Concept of the Generalized Reality-Orientation' in C. T. Tart (ed.) *Altered States of Consciousness* (Doubleday & Company Inc., 1969)
44. Springer, S. P. and Deutsch, G., *Left Brain, Right Brain* (W. H. Freeman and Company, 1981)

45. Tart, C. T., (ed.) *Altered States of Consciousness* (Doubleday & Company, Inc., 1969)
46. Thompson, R., *Foundations of Physiological Psychology* (Harper & Row, 1967)
47. Wagstaff, G. F., *Hypnosis, Compliance and Belief* (Harvester Press, 1981)
48. Wallace, B. and Fisher, L. E., *Consciousness and Behavior* (Allyn and Bacon, Inc., 1983)
49. Waxman, D., *Hypnosis* (Unwin Paperbacks, 1984)
50. White, R. A., 'A Preface to a theory of hypnotism,' *Journal of Abnormal and Social Psychology, Vol 36* (1941)
51. Wolberg, L. R., *Hypnosis. Is it for You?* (Harcourt Brace Jovanovich, Inc., 1972)

Index